Library of Congress Catalog Card Number: 99-90029

Publisher's Cataloging-in-Publication
(Provided by Quality books, Inc.)

Schacht, Rebecca.
    Lights along the path : Jewish folklore through
the grades / annotated, selected and retold by
Rebecca Schacht ; illustrated by Jacqui Morgan. --
1st ed.
    p. cm.
    Includes bibliographical references and index.
    SUMMARY: A graded collection of stories rooted
in ancient Jewish Talmudic and Midrash religious
sources.
    Audience: "Children age four to twelve."
    ISBN: 0-9668448-0-7

    1. Jews – Folklore. 2. Jewish folk literature.
3. Legends, Jewish. I. Morgan, Jacqui. II.
Title.

GR98.S34 1999   398'.089924
                  QBI99-290

The illustrations in this book were done in
transparent watercolor and inks on Arches paper.
The font used in the publication is Galliard.

Book and Cover Design by Susan Handman

Edited by Yael Gani

Chelsey Press
Beverly Hills, California

First Edition
Printed in Hong Kong

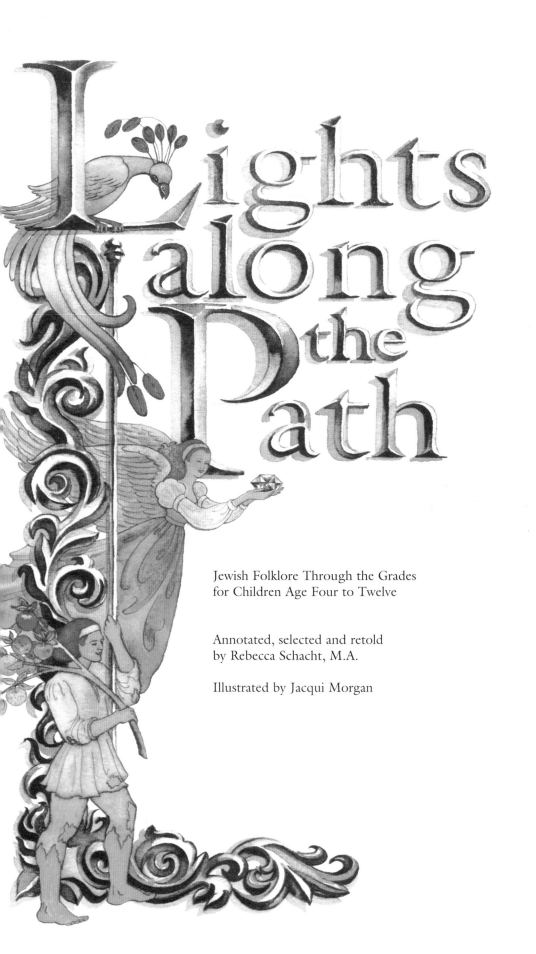

Lights along the Path

Jewish Folklore Through the Grades
for Children Age Four to Twelve

Annotated, selected and retold
by Rebecca Schacht, M.A.

Illustrated by Jacqui Morgan

This book is dedicated to Jeremy

In blessed memory of Ross Martin,
my beloved stepfather who introduced Jewish folk literature
to me with a book of Sholom Aleichem stories, and told
them to me with such love and artistry, that I understood them.

ACKNOWLEDGMENTS

I am deeply indebted to the gifted storytellers of the ages who have preserved the remarkable body of Jewish folklore from which I have had the privilege to select stories. The wisdom, humanity, and humor they have so beautifully preserved for mankind is my ongoing source of inspiration, admiration, and devotion. With great respect I retell the stories in the hope that new generations of children will benefit from discovering the unique treasures they contain.

With my lasting gratitude to:

Virginia Sease who, by example, taught me the process of becoming a teacher.

Yael Gani whose editorial expertise and insight enriched each page of the manuscript.

Susan Handman and Jacqui Morgan, whose enthusiasm, inspired designs and beautiful illustrations caught the spirit of the project.

Shirley Latessa, Jonathan Hilton, Walter Schacht, Olavee Martin, Joni Schacht, Marsie Scharlatt, Edward Sweeney, Claire Gerus, Ciella Goron-Wall, and in blessed memory, George Grindrod and Lois Parsons, for support and invaluable contributions in the preparation of this book.

Rabbi Joseph Telushkin for his masterful writings and spiritually inspiring services each month at the Synagogue for the Performing Arts in Los Angeles.

Elizabeth Stabler, Steve Seigel, 92nd St. Y Library, New York; Gabrielle Goldstein, Yeshiva University Library, New York; Susanne Kester, Skirball Museum, Skirball Cultural Center, Los Angeles, for generous resource assistance.

Contents

5

Kindergarten

First to Third Grades

First Grade

Second Grade

Fourth to Sixth Grades

SIXTH GRADE

She put the wings on and felt
their power as they beat back and
forth. Instantly, she knew how she
would return the precious jewel to
its proper place. She made a small
jump up, and away she flew.

— "Morning Star"

Foreword

Myth, legend, fable, fairy tale and folktale — this timeless body of literature, handed down by our ancestors, provides us with a view into our collective past. As we slip back in time to hear the stories that have been told through the ages, we access a window into our evolution. The stories illuminate our past, help us understand the present, and offer guidance for our future. This wondrous treasure should be cherished and carefully passed on to future generations.

The most effective way to pass this literary treasure on to our children is to read it to them. But when do we start? Which stories are most appropriate for our four-year-old child or our nine-year-old? This unique, lively, and colorful book is designed with these questions in mind. The story collection has been selected and arranged according to age and grade level, and is preceded by a brief overview of Jewish folk literature, and its value to children during the various developmental stages of their young lives.

The stories in *Lights along the Path* are rooted in ancient Talmudic and Midrash sources. Through character, setting, obstacle, and deed, the stories presented here offer aspects of Jewish culture, traditions, customs, and special wisdom. Some of the stories are familiar, some are obscure, and most contain motifs found in the folk literature of other cultures. Ever mindful of the warning by Howard Schwartz, author and preeminent folkloric scholar, that "modernizing" such tales can drain them of their soul, they have been altered as little as possible. Every effort was made to insure the integrity of each tale and its artistic form. It is important to note that these ancient stories are from a time in history that was not gender-sensitive, but every effort was made to make the text as inclusive as possible whenever appropriate within a given context. Idiomatic expressions, and Hebrew and Yiddish words are retained to maintain the original flavor of the stories.

Drawn from a world of miracles, where magic carpets soar, wise animals offer guidance, and people heroically transform themselves, these stories hold hope for solutions to human dilemmas. Each story has been chosen for meaning and genre suitable to a particular stage of development. The stories are told to entertain, educate, heal, and convey cultural values. As they explore both the real and the supersensible worlds, they often manifest psychological truths. Even as these particular fables, tales, and stories resonate from the soul of the Jewish people, they illuminate universal themes.

Today, multiculturalism is a primary goal in education. The aim of this inclusive approach is to value and support all cultures within our society. To know the struggles, hopes, and dreams of a people, through the voices heard in their literature, leads to greater cultural acceptance and appreciation. In the finest multicultural tradition, these stories foster friendships across cultural barriers and ultimately, because they are part of our human heritage, link us to each other.

Supported by current educational and psychological research, educators and psychologists seeking effective learning techniques and problem-solving strategies use the power of literature as a therapeutic tool. Jean Piaget, the eminent child psychologist, defined the different stages of a child's development and suggested different teaching modes to address each stage and each individual child. He believed that an education accenting the administration of a "system," rather than one focusing on a deeper understanding of the learner, undermines the child's spiritual and intellectual growth. Carl Jung and Jungian analysts have written comprehensively about the development of the individual as reflected through story. In *The Uses of Enchantment*, Bruno Bettelheim describes the irreplaceable value of folk literature to educate, support, and liberate the emotions of children at each psychological developmental stage. He maintains that the importance of fairy tales lies in their capacity to reveal the existence of powerful forces in a form that permits children to integrate them without trauma.

The international Waldorf School movement, founded by Rudolf Steiner, educator, scientist, and social philosopher, utilizes curricula based upon the developmental stages of children. The Waldorf curriculum begins by helping the child in the kindergarten years build a strong foundation for "creative fantasy" through play and story. Strong literature-based curriculum follows the child through each grade, as specific kinds of stories are introduced to meet the needs of the class and those of each individual child. The stories in this book have been selected on the basis of these guidelines.

As a classroom teacher, I find the stories to be a rich source of reference material to augment a full range of curricula — math, nature, ecology, social studies, language arts, history, geography, and science. Moreover, I find them invaluable as aids in working with emotional and behavioral issues. Instead of using the language of abstract thought and reasoned intellect, the stories speak to children out of an older "soul" language that creates a "once-upon-a-time" mood. In this mood, children of all ages and capabilities can understand and appreciate, at their own level, the psychological undertones and nuances within the stories. Through humor, self-reflection, and symbology the stories present imaginative "pictures" of the human condition. Just as the characters in theses ancient stories face hidden evils, fears that grip in the night, angry parents, jealous siblings, and the longing for a safe and happy place, today's child faces difficulties on his or her own path. With engaging insights, these tales can help chart the way for a less treacherous journey to adulthood.

There is an old Jewish tradition, stemming from the days when travel was dangerous, to clothe missions in good deeds. It is said that sending one into the world to do a good deed will ensure a safe journey. So to you, as a traveler about to embark on a literary journey, may you read and retell these stories as "good deeds," so that a protective shield of love and goodwill may surround you and all the children who hear them.

— REBECCA SCHACHT, 1999

Jewish Folk Literature

A Cultural Heritage

Jewish literature can be traced back to the founding of the Israelite religion in 1200 B.C.E. During the tenth century B.C.E., the Temple was built, the Hebrew alphabet was formed, and the idea of one God, or monotheism, became the cornerstone of Jewish belief. The stage was set for three thousand years of creative literature that reflects the history and values of the Jewish people. This body of literature offers us a unique and comprehensive view of the development of a people and its culture. Expressed through a variety of genres, Jewish literature is a vast, imaginative, and meaningful source from which to draw stories for children.

Professor Dov Noy, in *Folktales of Israel,* suggests that the typical Jewish tale has at least one of the four elements that will characterize its uniquely Jewish aspects. First, the story is likely to be set in time according to the Jewish calendar, often mentioning the Sabbath, festivals, rites of passage, birth, coming of age, marriage, or death. Second, a Jewish place — the synagogue, Israel, or a community — will be identified, often being threatened with annihilation. Third, the story will be peopled with Jewish characters.

Commonly found Jewish protagonists and heroes uncover plots to overthrow evil beings. The hero is often a *tzaddik,* "righteous man," whose wonder-working powers come from his knowledge of the Torah and his trust in God. The characters behave as "Jews," as understood by local society and custom. Fourth, is a message, a moral or lesson, often told by local sages or historical figures of biblical or post-biblical times. The lesson, usually about man's duty to God, to his people, or to his fellow man, is future-oriented, urging the listener to adopt an ideal or a goal, as yet unrealized, to improve his or her ways or acquire a new attitude.

The original sources for the stories in *Lights along the Path* are contained primarily in a body of classical Jewish rabbinical literature. This classical Judaism has predominated from ancient times to the present. Jewish tradition tells us that Moses received the Torah on Mount Sinai through God's revelation. The books of the Torah were given to Moses orally and in writing, and constitute Judaism's central document. They contain the stories of the patriarchs, Moses and the Exodus from Egypt, and the 613 commandments that form the basis for

15

Jewish law. This body of work is referred to as the Written Law.

Because God revealed himself also through "oral" teaching, the Torah, or Hebrew Bible, became more than just the written word. The truth of the Torah could be expressed through words, either written down or memorized, and through people — their physical gestures, and how they led their lives. Consequently, with Moses as their model, the ancient sages themselves became living embodiments of Torah. Their deeds served to reveal law, as much as their words expressed revelation. Their lives, memories, and gestures set standards that were included in the Torah as Oral Law. They became personifications of righteous and proper behavior for mankind to emulate. Upon this mystic premise many stories evolved.

Thus, the oral tradition begun at Mount Sinai was passed through the ages as the Torah was memorized by the great prophets, then sages, on down to the time of the masters at the beginning of the Common Era. These oral transmissions, with accompanying commentary called Mishnah, or Second Law, came to full expression in the definitive writing known as the Talmud. Rabbis began to write their commentaries on the Bible in the first centuries of the Common Era and completed the doctrine within the Jewish communities by about the fourth century. Their commentaries, or interpretations of the Mishnah, called Gemara, were included, and the entire document became known as the Palestinian, or Jerusalem, Talmud. Approximately a century later, the leading Babylonian rabbis added commentaries and did further editing, giving us what is known as the Babylonian Talmud. This Talmud became the most authoritative and remains the primary reference for classical Judaism.

Just as the Mishnah concerns itself with the normative rules of behavior and law (*halakha*), the Midrash, another Talmudic body of literature, concerns itself with norms of belief, virtue, right attitude and proper motivation. Told in narrative form, the Midrash stories, of an ethical and moral character, are called Aggadah, or lore. These stories literally "search out" the meanings and fill in the gaps between Scripture doctrine and rabbinical commentary, as they illuminate and explain the people and events of the Bible. This great body of historical and sacred literature is the foundation of Jewish folk literature. It consists of myths, legends, fables, fairy tales and folk tales containing religious "truths," anecdotes and moral maxims. This literary tradition continued growing for many hundreds of years until the Crusaders closed the Jewish schools in Babylonia at the end of the eleventh century.

Through the Torah, God formed a covenant with the Jews of Israel. The Torah guided the Jews in how they were to participate in the covenant, and specified how God would reward them. Rabbinical literature is filled with directions for working out the details of daily life in accordance with the covenant. To learn the Torah is to fulfill God's commandment. Thus, learning and study have always been held in especially high esteem in Jewish culture. The process of learning, including debate, memorization, and logic, was highly developed and set in motion centuries of valuing study, learning, and questioning. Every thought, action and deed of mankind and God was open to questioning. The earliest stories for children reflect these values. In the story "What is a Czar?" a boy learns about his environment by posing questions to his father. It is the questions themselves that are important. When the princess chooses a prince in "A Present for a Princess," the rationale for her decision is important. In "The Wise Maiden," the girl's logical thinking saves the king, and it is the Torah scholar in "The Orphan Boy..." who wins the bride!

The basic laws of Judaism have remained intact since Moses received the Written Law three thousand years ago. With the destruction of the Second Temple in 660 B.C.E., and the Roman occupation of Jerusalem in 70 B.C.E., the Jewish people were forced to maintain an identity for almost two thousand years without reliance upon a Temple or a homeland. They maintained their Jewish identity by following the basic laws, halakha, while adapting to or adopting the cultural traditions of the countries in which they lived. They continued to observe dietary laws *(kashrut)*, keep the Sabbath, practice circumcision, study Torah, and perform *mitzvot*, "divine commandments." These central and unifying acts are reflected throughout Jewish folk literature.

A vast amount of oral teaching and storytelling continued to develop as Jews observed and interpreted religious laws within each community and each family structure. This literature includes new traditions, as manifested in song, dress, food, and celebration. Each era brought new stories and new versions of old stories, all containing the threads of traditional messages. In the twelfth century, Berechiah ha-Nakdan, began writing down his own adaptations of animal tales, the *Fox Fables*. He adapted Aesop's fables to mirror Jewish culture by adding his own narrative details to the popular animal fables. His fables are filled with the language of the Torah, biblical quotations, and Jewish customs. In "The Moon in the Well," a fox lures a hungry wolf to a Jewish home preparing for the Sabbath; a mouse uses reason to subdue and teach a lion in "The Lion and the Mouse" and, in "The Fox and the Crow," a sly fox attempts to lure a crow by pretending to be a Torah scholar.

The Middle Ages gave rise to the most prolific period in Jewish folklore. Fairy tales and folktales became very popular. The legendary figures of early rabbinical literature were quite at home in the fairy-tale genre. Tales of good overcoming evil, traveling through supernatural or "other" worlds for the ultimate treasure, and the use of magical aids, are common themes and motifs. The great Jewish heroes from history are easily transformed into the kings and heroes of the fairy-tale realm, as we see in "King David and the Giant" and in "The Mysterious Palace." The many legends of Solomon and David are often embellished with fairy-tale motifs, without sacrificing their Jewish qualities. Solomon travels on his magic carpet to an ancient palace to discover new wisdom; David's battle with a giant is won with the aid of a magic mirror, a magic mare, and secret knowledge of the Name of God.

In the Middle Ages kabbalistic tales emerged, revealing a previously hidden mystical quality to Jewish literature. During the eighteenth century this mystical stream of literature flourished as the Hasidic movement in Eastern Europe developed around teachings of the charismatic Rabbi Israel Baal Shem Tov, "the Master of the Good Name." In "The Prophet Elijah Saves the Baal Shem Tov," we see how a revered ancient character, Elijah, is linked to the contemporary Baal Shem Tov, who was considered by his followers to know the "secrets of heaven." Tales of his wonderworks spread far and wide, leaving in their wake a devotional folk literature that is revered to this day. Professor Martin Buber's commentaries on Hasidism contributed to this mystical stream in the arts, inspiring contemporaries as diverse as Marc Chagall and Franz Kafka.

Rabbi Nachman of Bratslav, the greatgrandson of the Baal Shem Tov, continued in the tradition of mystical tales. He linked the symbolism in fairy tales to the magical imagery in the kabbalah and stressed the psychological and abstract concepts in Jewish literature. Rabbi Nachman saw the message of the Messiah on a cosmic scale as expressed through fairy tales.

In "The Lost Princess," when the viceroy searches for the princess, he must leave the earthly world and travel into the supernatural world in order to find and rescue her. Rabbi Nachman suggests that the lost princess, or soul, becomes that which must be sought after in each of us and that the journey, or quest, within the story represents personal restoration and redemption.

When oppression and hunger threatened the communities of Eastern Europe, rabbis were looked to for hope and salvation. Out of this climate came one of the most famous legends in Jewish lore, the legend of the golem — a man-like creature created by wonder-working rabbis with extraordinary powers to aid the Jewish community. In "The Golem of Vilna" a famous rabbi, the Gaon of Vilna, creates a golem to provide food for the Sabbath and fight life-threatening enemies.

Because Jewish folk literature is built upon the primacy of the Bible, it is the expression of monotheism, in contrast to the polytheism of other nations of antiquity, that often distinguishes it from the folk literature of other cultures. Values held within Jewish culture are always highlighted and expanded. The purpose of the stories is to explain the course of the universe and the destinies of mankind, to expose evil, and to form a relationship with God. Consequently, the stories are rich in moral imaginations and ethical ideas.

When Jewish folklore grapples with the forces of heaven and earth, paradise and hell, good and evil, the natural and the supernatural, the spiritual and the profane, several unifying and distinguishing features are found. They usually offer consolation and hope, invariably point out a moral lesson and, above all, they endeavor to inspire the readers and listeners with pride in their people and an implicit trust in God. In the Midrash tale, "The First Tear," it is an understanding God who sends a treasure to Adam and Eve to help them bear the pain of learning their earthly lessons.

Nobel Laureate Elie Wiesel writes the following regarding the characters in Jewish literature:

I try to show how all these characters are contemporaries. Their problems are our problems...their experience and their struggle are part of our conscience. We illustrate the human condition through them. Our legends aim to abolish the distance between one and the other. All Jewish legends and all Jewish figures try to help men live and survive in a stifling world where good and evil wear the same mask, where fire devours night and its shadows. Providing the food of friendship in a universe without warmth, that is the essence of these tales. All legends in Judaism have a common desire: to associate man with Creation and make him aware of the links with what surrounds him and preceded him. Destroy these links, destroy this consciousness, and man himself is destroyed, and so is his universe. For we are responsible for our beginning, which is our link to the mystery of Creation. In other words, legends of our times must be legends for all time and all men.

The *Lights along the Path* story collection begins with a creation midrash, "Alef is Chosen." In this story each Hebrew letter presents itself before God to state a case for its inclusion in the creation of the world. This tale, a lovely, imaginative picture for children containing many levels of interpretation, suggests that the letters existed before the world, that they are themselves holy, and that they are mysteriously linked to the creative process itself. The collection ends with the story "Moses Receives the Word of God." It tells of his mysterious journey through the heavens, then back to earth with the revelation. The stories in between tell of humankind living on the earth, posing the age-old questions: Where have I come from? What am I doing here? Where am I going? Jewish literature brings these basic questions to life in nursery rhymes, midrash, aggadah, folktales and fairy tales, fables, legends, and myths. This body of literature offers powerful "moral imaginations" for children on their own creative journey through the grades.

Folk Literature Through the Grades

There is a relation between the hours of our life and the centuries of time. The hours should be instructed by the ages and the ages explained by the hours.

— RALPH WALDO EMERSON

For thousands of years people have looked to divinely inspired sages to understand and navigate their world. The ancient wisdom of these sages has been handed down to us, age by age, through the grand and glorious mythologies of civilization. The common thread running through ancient mythology is an image of man descending from a spiritual homeland and developing upon the earth. Today these myths, now fragmented within each culture into legend, saga, fairy tale, and nursery rhyme, provide us with a rich legacy from our collective past. Reaching beyond science, this literature offers children aesthetic answers to questions of origin and creation.

Parents, educators, and child psychologists have come to recognize that developing children need the special kind of "nourishment" present in folk literature as much as they need physical sustenance. These stories provide children with what Waldorf educator H. Kugelen calls a "work space for their soul life." He maintains that literature offers a place where spiritual, emotional, and intellectual forces can be active, safe and non-confrontational. He further suggests that if we do not offer our children this imagery and special language, their "work spaces" will become filled with the trite and the ordinary and their souls will starve for knowledge of humanity's higher aims.

Robert Coles, Professor of Psychiatry and Medical Humanities at Harvard University, in his book *The Spiritual Life of Children*, writes about the effects on children of folk literature in general and of Bible stories in particular. He states:

Biblical stories...have a way of being used by children to look inward as well as upward. It should come as no surprise that the stories of Adam and Eve, Abraham and Isaac, Noah and the Ark, Abel and Cain, Samson and Delilah, David and Goliath, get linked in the minds of millions of children to their own personal stories as they explore the nature of sexuality and regard with awe, envy, or anger the power of their parents, as they wonder how solid and lasting their world is, as they struggle with brothers and sisters, as they imagine themselves as actual or potential lovers, or as actual or potential protagonists. The stories are not mere symbolism, giving expression to what people go through emotionally. Rather, I hear children embracing religious stories because they are quite literally inspiring — exciting their minds to further thought and fantasy and helping them become more grown, more contemplative and sure of themselves.

Through the grades, as a child's identity forms, folk literature provides multiple layers of meanings and "truths" about what it means to be human, and how and why to strive to be super-human. These messages, presented through imaginative pictures, events, experiences, and role models, are *most* valuable when discovered by children for themselves. The child may recognize the message of a story immediately, or the message may enter the child's mind like a seed that will grow at some time in the future.

As those who read to children search the stories for symbolic meaning, spiritual or psychological, their own curiosity and symbol-forming powers will be awakened and they will find previously hidden layers of meaning that do convey universal truths. When the reader respects the heritage of the tales, and understands the special language of folk literature, the emotional impact of any given story becomes extremely potent for the child.

Sigmund Freud, Carl Jung, and Joseph Campbell have analyzed the picture-language and symbolism of folk literature and have determined that it is helpful in exploring the landscape of the unconscious. Bruno Bettelheim, in *The Uses of Enchantment*, attributes the current adult craving for fantasy stories, quests, sagas, and science fiction to "fairy-tale starvation." Julius Heuscher, in *A Psychiatric Study of Myths and Fairy Tales,* suggests using folk literature for children as an aid to emotional growth and the individuation process.

Babies are born into a complex environment that they must perceive and organize. In the process of perceiving, organizing and learning to adapt, a foundation is formed from which their thinking skills, emotional life, and physical actions will later develop. We watch in wonder as they eat, sleep, grow, and appear to change before our eyes. They appear to experience their environment with their whole beings as their eyes, ears, hands and feet move in reaction to our voices, sounds, and other environmental stimuli.

The soft, rhythmical tunes of lullabies are usually our children's first literary experience. Lullabies encourage babies to practice sounds, rhythmic patterns, and movement. During the first year a child learns to make the sounds of language, followed by words. Soon thereafter, a magical moment occurs when the child enters the stage of "naming." Naming is a purely human act that goes far beyond repeating sounds or saying words. By naming, babies make statements of fact about the world outside of themselves. They delight at learning names because they've built a bridge that connects them to the world. Out of themselves, they've communicated to another, and have been recognized. This exciting moment is recapitulated in the story of Adam naming the wild beasts and birds of the earth. The story remains a source of pleasure every time a child hears it.

Closely tied to naming is the child's capacity for memory, the first prerequisite to thinking. As children practice speech, and recall names by memory, a foundation for their future thinking capacity is developed. When a child's speech starts to include adjectives and verbs, he or she first encounters grammar, and the second prerequisite to thinking is established. Here, in the logic of language and grammar, the rules of reason take precedence and a foundation for common sense and reasoning is laid.

After place and spatial memory have been established in the child's first year, and time and speech memories have developed in the second year, a picture memory process begins. Jean Piaget refers to this stage and describes how a child begins to remember objects that are out of sight. This is demonstrated in the delightful game of peekaboo. Perceptions and conceptualizations begin to connect with the child's experiences through this picture memory. A child can hold the memory picture sequence of experiences together by exercising his or her individual "self," or "I." Gradually, as the child's "I" forms these picture memories, then sequences them into ideas, thinking is born.

With thinking, a child begins the gradual and sometimes difficult process of separating from a "oneness" with the world, into an individual "self," separate from the surrounding environment. This individuation, or "self" evolvement process, begun in the child's first three years, continues through the early elementary school grades. As children accumulate experiences of the world, and then remember them through their picture memories, they build their own, unique knowledge base from which to form ideas into thinking. At each stage of development another world of ideas opens up and the child must form new unions with the world. This knowledge base, and the kind of relationship a child forms with the world, is greatly influenced by the literature we present to them through the grades.

The stories in this collection have been specifically chosen to recapitulate earlier gains in a child's development, to support existing inner developmental activity, and to serve as seeds that will blossom in the child's future. The stories suggested for specific grades are appropriate, but are not intended to be limiting. "Moses Receives the Word of God" would be as beautiful and as fitting in the third grade as in the sixth. "Morning Star," a kindergarten fairy tale, could serve to introduce astronomy to fifth graders. The stories are culturally and pedagogically so valuable that they can be used through the grades at many different times, depending on the motives of the readers, and the needs and interests of the young listeners.

This collection of stories follows Waldorf education guidelines for story criteria and genre selection for each grade. In the Waldorf curriculum, designed for kindergarten through high school students, every classroom subject is brought to life through the use of literature. Over and over, the themes of transformation and enchantment, release and redemption, tell of human trials and ways of reaching goals, and of solving problems. The teachers artistically incorporate these themes into all subjects in order to engage the students and connect them in a living way to the curriculum, and to the accumulated experience of humankind.

Today we can discover anew the artistic and psychological treasures our folk literature contains. These ancient stories with their archetypes and primal human memories, what Jung calls the "collective unconscious," remain timeless. Like the child, we take from stories what our times dictate. We find our children reflected in the protagonist starting upon a journey into the forest and meeting the loyal huntsman, the helpful giant, the wicked witch, or the wise old sage. We long to help them get to the enchanted palace safely, to join the king and queen in the celebration of the wedding of the prince and princess, and to "live happily ever after."

Kindergarten
Ages Four to Six

The prince must rise at dawn and go into the palace garden... He must put on his coat and take with him a bottle of water and a knife. In the garden he will find three pumpkins growing on a single vine.

— "The Princess of the Third Pumpkin"

"When did it happen, where did it happen, when and where did it not happen?" This is the kind of question a Waldorf teacher will use to begin to tell a fairy tale to a kindergarten class. The question serves to set a tone and mood for the children. When the room quiets, the teacher begins, and as the story unfolds the children are transported into a fairy tale world where an imaginative and exciting adventure awaits them.

Literature in the kindergarten years should first and foremost enrich and enliven every aspect of the children's world of play and fantasy. Play strengthens their previous developmental gains and lays the foundation for their future thinking capacity. Through play and fantasy the child's speaking is activated, the memory strengthened, and the "I" is awakened. In the kindergarten years the child is still in the early stages of transition from a "oneness" with the world into an individual in the world. As play calls upon the "I" organization within the child to direct play activities, the process will exercise and encourage the child's growing sense of "self." When children have a vast repertoire of ideas to incorporate into active playing and fantasizing, their play becomes beneficial and more meaningful to them. The more imaginative their world of play becomes, the better their "inner workspace" is for the process of individuation and the establishment of union with their environment.

Ideal stories for this age are those in which the fundamental laws of the fairy-tale world prevail. It is in this world — where kindly beings help you if you try to do right, growth comes through trials and mistakes, forgiveness follows true repentance, and good always wins in the end — that the best material to stimulate imaginative play and fantasy is found. It is in these fairy tales that the evil wrought by trolls, witches, dragons and giants serves to spur the hero to greater efforts, and it is here that obstacles are overcome with the help of the good forces. This attitude of positive thinking is natural to healthy children and beneficial to children with emotional and/or adjustment problems.

Animals and inanimate objects often speak in stories for kindergarten children. These talking animals, flowers, stones, or raindrops are accepted because it's the way children still experience the world. The story action immediately engages and entertains the child. The deeper meanings in the tales can be experienced if and when the child needs them. In "The Old Crone and The Little Girl," the conversation between the twirling animals and objects sets a magical scene in which the environment is alive and meaningful, and the sequence of events is entertaining and humorous. In "The Bear's Bellyache," the children are saved from the bear's tummy by their parents, and all watch happily as the bear lumbers off into the woods holding his belly, singing about "bones and stones." The child will transform these fantasy pictures, lively words, and clearly drawn characters into imaginative play experience. The deeper meanings, good prevailing over evil, obedience to one's parents, the terror of being left alone, may be explored or understood when the child is ready, but the goal of enlivened play through meaningful stories has been achieved.

Because fairy tales can be understood and enjoyed on several levels, repetition of the stories is a good idea and is appreciated by both the younger and older kindergartners. Familiar characters become friends who can be counted on to act in a certain manner, and the celebrations at the end of the stories are always a satisfying experience. In the tale of "The Princess of the Third Pumpkin," spells, magic potions, and enchantments must be overcome before the prince identifies his true princess. In "The Lost Princess," the beautiful tale of love and faithfulness righting a wrong, a willful princess is banished to the devil by her angry father, the king. He sends his trusty viceroy into the supernatural world to save her. In "Morning Star," a young girl bravely outwits a demon. These stories incorporate the requisite fairy tale elements and provide meaningful concepts for the child to grow into.

Jewish literature has given us another kind of folktale, one that is loved for its element of repetition. It is a far-fetched, humorous tale told in a continuous flow of contradictions. "What Is a Czar?" is a good example of such a tale. As children learn about and adapt to their environment, these lively tales give them colorful words to describe what they see, do, and feel.

Also important are tales that show the consequences of powerful growth forces or emotions out of control. The required restraint is then acquired through the guidance, comfort and understanding of adult figures. As the waters threaten in "The Secret of Power," God responds by sending tiny grains of sand to restore harmony in nature. In "The First Tear," God sends the treasure of tears to help Adam and Eve as they learn their painful lessons on earth. In "Alef is Chosen," a tiny, shy letter receives a special place in the creation of the universe. As they create dramatic images, these stories offer comforting messages for children feeling alone, helpless or insignificant.

Scholars have come to agree that the first poem ever published with children's needs in mind is "One Only Kid — Had Gadya." This poem of unknown origin, but traced back to the ninth century, was first published in 1590 in Prague. In the centuries following, the tale has been enjoyed as a riddle, a symbolic fable, an allegory, and a song, and has a special place in the Haggadah for the Passover feast, the *seder*. This simple tale incorporates the ideal elements for kindergarten children: a quest for the most powerful entity in the universal hierarchy, an interpretive potential in its message, and lively entertainment value.

First Grade

The heavens He created from the light of His Garment.

— "THE FIRST DAY OF CREATION"

Folk literature in the first grade should give children an all-encompassing overview of their world through large, imaginative pictures and uncomplicated time sequences. Creation stories with universal cosmic pictures that portray powerful elemental forces are ideal. Because individual human trials are not yet in a child's area of interest, stories that are on a grander scale than a child's own life experience are most appealing.

Many folk stories and fairy tales can now be directly related to the first-grade curriculum as the academic concepts of numbers, reading, and writing are introduced. Especially good are stories that amplify and bring to life aspects of nature — earth, air, fire, and water. Plants and animals can demonstrate the human qualities of courage, honesty, warmth of heart, and kindness. Trickery, treachery, cruelty, and folly — as personified in witches, giants, or dragons — are other aspects of human nature that can be safely viewed through clearly drawn characters. In the "Witches of Ashkelon," we hear about a clever rabbi who tricks the wicked witches into dancing in the rain in order to break their spells. Each witch gets a punishment to fit her misdeed.

Second Grade

Once upon a time a fox said to a wolf, "I have an excellent suggestion for you if you want to enjoy a really delicious meal. But you must follow my instructions very carefully."

— "THE MOON IN THE WELL"

Animal fables can be fully appreciated by second graders. Because this is a puzzle- and riddle-loving age, the fables give children an opportunity to sharpen their wits on the logic of the animals, and have fun recognizing human characteristics in the respective temperaments of various species. If children are allowed to discover for themselves the benefits of reason and kindness ("The Lion and the Mouse"), the consequences of greed ("The Dog's Reflection"), or the idea that help will come when we try to do the right thing ("The Rabbi and the Lion"), the lessons will long be remembered.

The perfect balance to animal fables, actually one-sided human nature stories, are legends of holy men and saints. While animal characters mirror man at his most basic, the miracle workers transcend even the more fully realized human being. These characters display the finest human qualities of love and wisdom. The "Golem of Vilna" offers just such a legend, as the wise rabbi creates a man-like creature to come to the aid of the community when hunger and oppression threaten.

Stories can now have a more complicated variation of plot and feeling, with contrast and conflict between good and evil — the evil sketched in lightly, good always prevailing, and errors corrected and forgiven. Sequence tales are important to exercise both memory and clear thinking skills.

Third Grade

Abram, look to the east, look to the west, look to the north, and look to the south. All the land that you see I give to you and your children forever. Rise and walk the distance of this land for it belongs to you.

— GOD'S MESSAGE IN "THE STORY OF ABRAHAM"

Bible stories that describe the journey of mankind from paradise to earth are especially well-suited for third graders. These stories reflect the journey a child makes from the dreamy imaginative world of childhood into the denser earthly world of matter. At this age, as children's self-consciousness deepens and their egos strengthen, a more aggressive willfulness appears in their behaviors. The Bible characters resemble this willful, defiant time through their actions and their struggles with restrictions. Eve's disobedience of God, the sins of Cain, Noah's heroic efforts, and David's battle with Goliath clearly illustrate this rebellious phase. As the complex concepts of individual responsibility and conscience begin to stir, the warnings of the prophets speak directly to these subtle moral crises within the child.

During this stage of development, children can understand their own responsibility for the effect their actions have upon others. In "The Two Brothers," human kindness is illustrated as each brother puts the needs of the other before his own. The idea of responsibility for actions, which brings a new measure of freedom, becomes a more grown-up garment for the evolving "I." With this capacity, children can now engage in reasoned arguments about right and wrong. They can accept an objective code of behavior, just as the Israelites accepted the Ten Commandments.

Growing up can become a lonely experience as a child seeks an independent life and tries to establish relationships with authority figures. These experiences are beautifully paralleled in the Israelites' struggle with God. The stories of strong divine guidance in the Bible can be comforting to children. The encouragement the stories offer can allay fears and bring renewed enthusiasm for action. Stories in which the hero forgets how to act, struggles, then tries again are ideal. In "The Mysterious Palace," we find that even the wise King Solomon must relearn lessons and change his ways. In "King David and the Giant," we find another heroic king in danger, but with the use of his magic objects everything turns out well in the end.

Children can now fully grasp the concept that time is organized and is perceived as past, present, and future. With this understanding, their objective consciousness can accept the idea that what was done yesterday will bring consequences at a future time. Stories set in ancient times give a sense of history, and village settings speak to a child's dawning awareness of community life. This is illustrated in "The Story of Abraham," as the great Jewish patriarch leads his people to settle a nation.

Fourth Grade

… Solomon found himself in a strange and foreign place. Without his magic ring, his powers were gone, his wisdom was gone, and he was penniless. He wandered from city to city, begging from door to door. He told everyone he met that he was Solomon, the King of Israel. But the people laughed…

— "King Solomon and Ashmodai"

At the age of nine, a crucial point is reached in a child's development. The dreamy "once-upon-a-time" world is left behind as a child's consciousness becomes more objective, and he or she emerges as a citizen of the world. Especially valuable to children experiencing these powerful inner growth forces are epics and great sagas with clearly defined heroic men and women who grow and change from their deeds and misdeeds, and from the trials they endure while finding their way.

Literature that promotes a careful and accurate observation of the world is important in the fourth grade. In "The Flaw on the Diamond," a deep scratch ruins a valuable diamond, only to become more valuable through the talents of an expert diamond cutter. In "A Fortune for Chelm," a humorous tale from the infamous village of Chelm, the reasoning skills of the students will be challenged. Language arts, drawing, math, science, social studies, geography, and ecology lessons can all be brought to life through folk stories.

Fifth Grade

Where you go, I will go; where you sleep, I will sleep; where you die, I will die. Your people are my people; your God is my God. I swear by the God of Israel that only death shall separate me from you!

— "The Story of Ruth"

Although still working through some aspects of the individuation process, most ten-year-olds enter into a time of balance — referred to by Waldorf educators as "a golden balance"— between childhood and adolescence. Folk literature with a realistic, factual basis is most beneficial as students explore the great civilizations of Ancient Egypt, Persia, Babylonia, Greece and Rome. Mythologies of these ancient cultures tell us that divine guidance was sought and received by humankind. Jewish stories, traced to these cultures, offer colorful and imaginative pictures about other peoples and other times.

As ten-year-old children are ready to move into the greater community as individuals, biographies with concrete fact, using direct quotation, help children develop the skills to separate fact, fiction, and opinion. In "The Story of Ruth," we travel with Ruth as she bravely moves into a new social context. Stories containing elements of history, such as "Alexander in Jerusalem" and "King Ptolemy and the Torah," bring history to life and make it meaningful for students. Also important are fanciful stories of people using their wits to solve problems, escape danger, or help those in their communities. In the wisdom riddle tale "The Wise Maiden," a young woman employs logical thinking when she is called upon to unravel a mystery for the king.

Sixth Grade

The young man slept on the branches high up in the tree until a soft breeze awakened him. Startled, he looked around and saw that all the apples in the tree had turned to stones on which beautiful Hebrew letters appeared.

— "The Orphan Boy Who Won the Bride"

By the sixth grade children have journeyed through childhood, experienced a moment of "golden balance," and are preparing to step into adolescence. This brings a new set of questions regarding identity, self-esteem, and social conduct. This is the time to help them establish a strong moral code by providing images that will help them confidently know themselves as individuals. Stories with pictorial representations to inspire and serve as models are excellent during this stage of a child's development. Such stories contain quests for knowledge, and clear themes of right and wrong — heroes fighting honorable battles, adherence to moral codes, or righteous men and women performing good deeds.

Stories of explorers, of present-day heroes, and stories filled with logic and humor serve to prepare, guide, and provide resources from which these students can draw. "Rabbinical Math" poses a problem of fairness that children will enjoy solving as they match their own logic and mathematical skills with those of the rabbi. They will understand the subtle irony in the tzaddik's dream in "The Location of Paradise," and will take special delight in "The Orphan Boy Who Won the Bride," wherein the poor boy, by virtue of his acquired knowledge, wins the treasured bride.

Moses is considered the model of the righteous human being. In "Moses Receives the Word of God," he travels on an arduous journey through the heavens to accept the Commandments from God, then brings them back to the Israelites. Two thousand years later, in the historically based "King Ptolemy and the Torah," Ptolemy tests the sages on their interpretations of these same laws. These stories challenge listeners to think about their own moral ideas. Debate and discussion can emanate from every question asked by the king, and from every answer given by the sages. The image of the sages laboring to interpret the Word of God, to provide mankind with guidelines and laws to govern life on earth, is a strong example to set for sixth graders as they form a moral code for themselves.

*The prince must rise at dawn
and go into the palace garden...
In the garden he will find
three pumpkins growing on a
single vine... from one of these
pumpkins will emerge the most
beautiful princess in the whole
world.*

— "The Princess of the Third Pumpkin"

Kindergarten

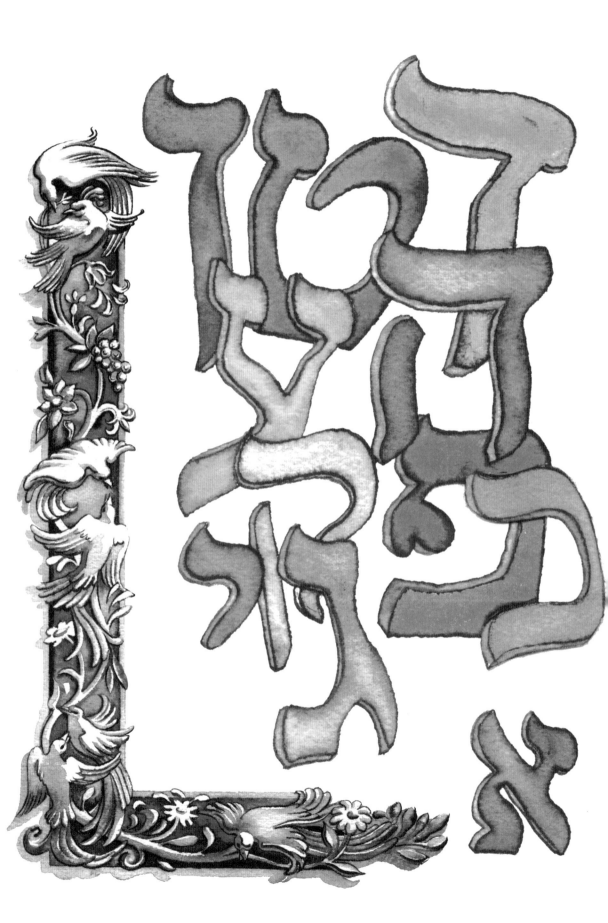

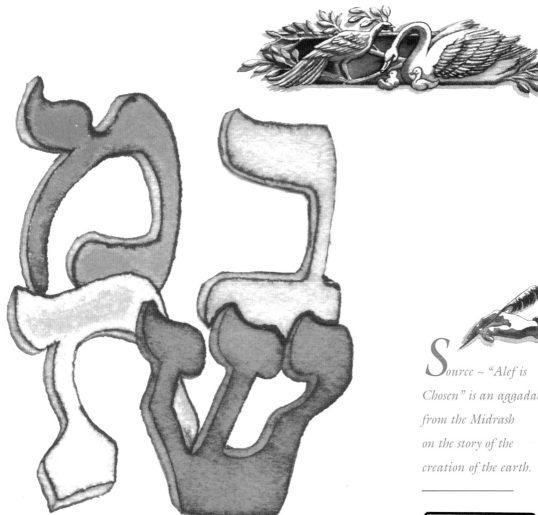

Alef is Chosen

Twenty-two generations before the creation of the world, God sat on the magnificent Throne of Glory and consulted His plans for the creation of the world. Around the base of his great crown, engraved with a pen of flaming fire, were the twenty-two letters of the Hebrew alphabet. Each letter wanted to be part of God's creation. So one by one, the letters wriggled and squirmed and worked their way out of the Holy Crown to come down and stand before God. They tumbled and

*S*ource ~ *"Alef is Chosen"* is an aggadah from the Midrash on the story of the creation of the earth.

The Hebrew alphabet, the Alefbet, is written from right to left.

God divinely ordained the letters, each is sacred. Attributed to each letter are a graphic form, a numerical value, and symbolic meanings.

— PSALMS 119

jostled and pushed each other about as they tried to win the attention of Father God. Each letter cried out, "Almighty God, create the world through me."

The first bold letter to push to the front to stand before God was Tav. "I have the best reason for wanting to be chosen to lead the creation of the world," said Tav. "My letter stands at the beginning of the word 'Torah.'"

"This is true, Tav," replied God. "And in 3,306 years' time, I shall give Moses the Torah as my Word for the children of Israel."

Tav was consoled by God's words and quietly retreated.

Then Bet, the second letter of the alphabet, came before the Throne. Speaking to God, Bet said, "O Lord God, I stand at the beginning of the daily prayer in Your praise, which begins with *Baruch...* 'Blessed be the Lord forever.' Surely, this suggests that I should be used to head your new creation."

And the Lord God was pleased with these words and took the letter Bet and placed it as the first letter of the Hebrew words *bereshit bara...*, "In the Beginning He Created..."

Then, one by one, the other letters of the alphabet pleaded their cases before God. Each explained why it, above all others, should stand at the beginning of the creation of the world. God listened patiently to each presentation.

God noticed that the letter Alef did not enter into the competition with the others, but remained quietly at the side. "Alef, why is it that you are standing so quietly, and why are you the only one who has asked nothing of me?"

"Lord God of the Universe," answered Alef, "I am

the least among Your letters. Since my number value is only one it is not right for me to make any demands upon You."

God was very impressed with the modesty shown by Alef and said, "Because you are so cautious in putting yourself forward, and feel yourself to have such little value, it is you who shall be first among the letters, you will lead the alphabet. It is true that your value is one, but God is One, and the Torah is also One. When my people receive the Ten Commandments, which are the essence of the Torah, I will honor you by using your name to introduce them."

And so the letter Alef is pronounced first in the Hebrew alphabet and first in the word *Anochi*, "I am the Lord Thy God."

A charming tradition is practiced to this day in Jewish schools when children are introduced to the alphabet — a drop of honey is placed on the page with the letters, or honey cakes are passed to the class, so they will always remember the sweetness of learning.

Alef אָ, *the first letter of the alphabet, has a value of one and is the symbol of God's oneness. Alef begins the name of Adam, the first human being in the Bible.*

The Rosebush
and the Apple Tree

Long ago in a lovely garden grew a beautiful rosebush. Next to it grew an apple tree. One day, when the rosebush was in full bloom, everyone who passed by commented on its exquisite beauty and its glorious scent. The rosebush

heard the compliments and lavished in the adoration it was receiving. The rosebush liked the attention so much that it became quite vain and conceited.

"Don't you think it is *I* who is the most important in the garden?" the rosebush bragged to the apple tree one day. "Just look around, none can compare with my beauty. My blossoms are the most fragrant in the garden. And though some, like you, are much larger, I am the prettiest and give the most pleasure to everyone."

The apple tree looked over the entire garden, and then said to the rosebush, "You are indeed very beautiful, but no matter how beautiful you are and no matter how sweet your blossoms, I don't think it is you who is the most important."

"What do you mean?" snapped the rosebush.

"I think the most important in the garden is the one who is the most kindhearted," replied the apple tree. "And in this respect you can't be compared with me."

"Do tell, apple tree!" said the offended rosebush. "How is it that you think you are so kindhearted, and that I lack this virtue of which you are so proud?"

"Watch," said the apple tree.

A group of children who were playing in the garden approached the apple tree. One of them picked up a stone and tossed it at the tree, aiming at a large red apple. The stone missed the apple, hit a branch and shook the tree. Many apples fell to the ground. The children cheered, gathered the apples, and ran off to continue their games. One child stopped at the rosebush. She reached into the bush to pick a flower and was pricked on her finger by a thorn.

"Now do you understand?" asked the apple tree. "For you to give away your sweet flowers, you must first prick a person with your thorns, but I give my delicious fruit even to those who throw stones at me."

Source ~"The Rosebush and the Apple Tree" is a Midrashic parable from the first century.

In Jewish literature, the Garden of Eden, a garden, or the trees in a garden often symbolize the feminine aspect of the Divine Presence, or "Shekhinah."

"A word fitly spoken is like apples of gold in pictures of silver."
— PROVERBS 25:11

What Is a Czar?

Long ago, when an almighty czar ruled Russia, children listened wide-eyed to the tales their parents told of this great ruler. During the long, cold winter nights of Eastern Europe, as families gathered around warm stoves, children listened to stories of the czar's victorious battles, the vast country he ruled, his enormous estates, and his fabulous treasures. But the tales children liked best were about the strange habits of the czar. The children begged for more and more details, so these stories grew, becoming more and more wondrous with each telling.

On a cold snowy night, a young boy sat by the stove warming his hands. As his father added wood to the fire, the boy asked to hear a story about the czar. "Which story would you like to hear?" asked the father.

"There are many things that I've heard about him," replied the boy, "but I want you to tell me what really makes a czar a czar. In the village they say that the czar is so powerful that the ocean itself changes when he goes in for a swim. The water turns to just the right temperature for him — never too hot, never too cold. Do you think this could be true?"

"My dear son, the great oceans are the same for everyone; the water does not change. If the water is cold for you, it is cold for the czar." Then the father paused, stroked his beard, and added, "But, of course, when the czar goes in the water it is different because, as we all know, the czar is a czar."

Source ~ "What Is a Czar?" is a folktale from the oral tradition of nineteenth-century Russia. It is a tale that introduces the riddle genre.

The word czar is a derivation of Caesar, the name of many ancient Roman rulers.

"Oh yes, father. I also heard that the czar wears a magic bathing suit, one made of a material that is dry when he comes out of the water. Is this true?"

"No, no, my boy, this is not at all true. These are just tales. You should not believe them. When the czar comes out of the water, he is just the same as you are when you come out of the water — wet." Then the boy's father held up his hand and added, "But wait, when the czar comes out of the water, it is, of course, different, he is a czar, and the czar is a czar."

The boy pressed on, "And they say that when the czar is sick the great doctors from all parts of the world come to heal him. And these great miracle workers are able to keep the Angel of Death away so that the czar will never die. Could this be true?"

The father shook his head, "Oh no, my child, that is definitely not true. Of course, when the czar is sick, all the greatest doctors do come to him, and they do stand between him and the Angel of Death, but the best that any miracle worker can do is make the Angel of Death wait. We all know that the Angel of Death will eventually win every man. So even the great czar will die one day, just as you and I will one day die." The father became thoughtful for a moment, and then added, "But, of course, the czar is different."

"Father," the boy went on, "what about the czar's food? What things can a czar eat? They say that his food is not like ours."

Patting the boy's head, the father said, "His food is just like ours, but there is a difference. He is a czar."

Puzzled, the boy said, "What about bread? Is his bread like ours?"

"Oh yes, the czar eats a lot of bread, but it is not quite like our bread. It is different, for he is a czar."

"Father, what about potatoes?" asked the boy. "They say the czar doesn't open his mouth to put the potatoes in with a fork as we do. They say he opens his mouth wide, and that his servants stand in a very long line and toss the potatoes in, one after another, faster and faster."

"Oh no, no, my son, the czar eats potatoes just as we do, but they are not quite like our potatoes. They are different, for he is a czar."

"Father, does the czar eat eggs?" asked the boy.

"Yes, he eats eggs just as we do, but of course the eggs are not like our eggs, they are different, for he is a czar."

"Do his cows give him milk to drink, as ours do?"

"He drinks milk, but it is not like our milk. He is a czar, and the czar is different."

"They say that when the czar drinks tea he doesn't put it in a cup and add sugar as we do, but that he pours it into a large sugar bowl, then drinks it. Is this true?"

"No, but he does drink his tea differently, because he is a czar."

"Is the czar big, like a giant?"

"No, no, my son. He has a body just like all men — two legs, two eyes, two arms, one nose, one mouth — just as you have. But always keep in mind that the czar is a czar, not quite like you and me."

The boy sighed, "Well, now at last I understand what a czar is."

"And what is that?" asked the father.

Smiling, the boy said, "The czar is the same as we, but a czar is a czar, so that at the same time that he is like us, he is different."

"Yes, my boy," said the father, stoking the fire, "You do understand."

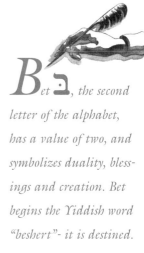

Bet בּ, the second letter of the alphabet, has a value of two, and symbolizes duality, blessings and creation. Bet begins the Yiddish word "beshert"- it is destined.

*S*ource ~ "The
Bear's Bellyache"
is a folktale from
the oral tradition
of mid-nineteenth-
century Russia.

The Bear's Bellyache

Once upon a time, in a tiny cottage near the edge of a great forest, there lived a rabbi with his wife and their six children. One day, when the rabbi was at the synagogue and his wife was in the village marketing, a huge brown bear came to the cottage. He pounded and

pounded on the door until he finally broke it in. He went into the cottage, gathered up all the children, and ate them for lunch. The bear lumbered off into the forest feeling full and content. He soon became very tired and fell asleep.

Later that day, when the rabbi and his wife returned to the cottage, they discovered that their children were gone. They looked everywhere.

"Where are you, dear children?" they called as they searched and searched.

"Father, Mother, we are here, inside the bear!" came the voices from the forest. "He ate us for lunch! Please come quick!"

The rabbi thought of a plan to save his children. He and his wife went into the forest, cautiously approached the bear, and gently woke him.

"Bear," said the rabbi, "Why don't you come to our house and let me pick those nasty lice out of your fur. You will feel much more comfortable."

"No," said the bear as he started to go. "I will not come to your house."

"Oh, please come," said the rabbi's wife. "I'll give you a bowl of cereal."

"No, I won't come," said the bear over his shoulder, as he moved deeper into the forest.

The rabbi's wife continued, "I'll give you a delicious bowl of cereal with butter."

Again the bear answered, "No, I will not come." He was almost out of sight.

"We'll add some meat for you," added the rabbi.

"Meat!" exclaimed the bear as he stopped and turned. "For meat, I'll come!" And he followed the rabbi and his wife back to the cottage.

The bear seated himself at the table while the

rabbi's wife prepared her finest stew. She gave the bear as much as he could eat. And eat and eat he did! Bowls and bowls, until he was so full that he couldn't move. He put his head down on the table and fell asleep. The rabbi quickly grabbed a huge knife, cut open the bear's belly, took out all of his children, and kissed them one by one.

After the rabbi and his wife had washed, scrubbed, and given cereal to each of the children, they carefully hid them. They put one behind the chair, one under the table, one in the bed, one under the bed, one beside the clay oven, and they hid the tiniest child in a big pot on the stove.

While the bear was still asleep, the rabbi and his wife filled his stomach with stones and bones, and then quickly sewed him up. The bear woke up just after they had finished. He grabbed his stomach and felt the heavy stones and bones. Oh, what a terrible bellyache he had! Moaning and groaning, he lumbered off into the forest, singing this song as he went:

"Tra, la-laa, tra, la-lee
I feel I've got bones
and big heavy stones
Rattling in my bell-eeeee."

The rabbi's wife probably lured the bear with "cholent," a potted meat and vegetable dish, traditionally cooked on Friday and simmered overnight for the Sabbath noonday meal.

The First Tear

In the days after Adam and Eve had been banished from the Garden of Eden they wandered the earth, feeling lost. They thought about what they had done

and what was now to happen to them. They were sorry for their mistakes, and grew very sad. Father God watched them with great compassion. He understood how they were feeling. He knew how deeply they missed the beautiful Garden of Eden, and how hard their life on earth would be. He thought of something that would help them.

Father God spoke to Adam and Eve. "Dearest children," he said gently, "I understand your sorrow and I am very sorry that you must suffer in this way. I understand that you miss your beautiful garden. But because you did not follow my commandments, you must now live upon the earth. You had to leave the beautiful garden where you were taken care of and lived in peace. Now you will learn the great lessons of earth. The price you have paid for these lessons is very high. The sorrow you must endure has only begun; there is much more ahead of you. I cannot offer you protection from these painful lessons, but I can assure you that I will hold you in my thoughts at all times, and that my love for you will never end. The reward for lessons learned is wisdom. Every difficulty that you encounter and each heartache you feel contains an important lesson. Because your struggles will at times overwhelm you, I have decided to present you with a treasure that will help you through the painful and difficult times that lie ahead. This heavenly gift will come to you in the form of a pearl."

"Look at the pearl carefully. Hold it tenderly. Whenever sadness and grief overcome you, and you feel that your heart is about to break, this tiny pearl will fall from your eyes as a tear! When it falls, something will change inside you, making you feel lighter and less lonely. You may have as many tears as you wish and they will last your whole life long."

Source ~ "The First Tear" is a parable from the Midrash.

Legend says Adam received the first book, the Book of Raziel, from the angel Raziel. The book told Adam of all the future generations of the earth.

Source ~ "The Secret of Power" is a parable from the Midrash.

In Jewish folklore water is often a symbol for Torah knowledge.

The Secret of Power

The Almighty God sat on His great Throne in heaven and surveyed His creations. Water, one of His creations, came swooshing and swirling into heaven and rose until it touched the very Throne of Glory. The Almighty, concerned that water was acting improperly, cried out a warning: "Stop, you have come too far, and

you are behaving in a manner dangerous to everything that is around you."

But the waters had become prideful and would not listen to the Almighty. They even boasted: "We are the mightiest creation of all. We can go upon the earth and cover all the lands with great floods. Of all Your creations, we are the most powerful."

The waters' lofty boasting angered the Almighty. He promised they would be taught a lesson about the danger of their pride and showing off their brute force. He shook His fist at the waters, and His booming voice cried out, "You may not threaten to control the earth!"

The Almighty gathered grains of sand from the four corners of the earth and told them how to join together. He then sent an angel to accompany the tiny grains of sand to earth to meet the raging waters.

When the waters saw the tiny grains they laughed and teased the sand. "Did Father God really think that you tiny specks could stand up against us, the mighty waters? You silly little fools! We will send our smallest wave to sweep over you. In just one second you'll be gone."

When the tiny grains of sand heard the powerful threat of the waters, they became frightened. "Have no fear, dear grains of sand," said their angel. "It is true that you are tiny. If the waters wash over you when you are alone, you will not be able to protect yourselves. But hold fast, you need only remain united. The waters will come to understand your strength."

The little grains of sand heeded the words of the angel and were comforted by them. Soon the winds blew the sands from all the lands of the earth. The grains gathered together, one on top of the other. As they clung to one another, they began to form into beaches

beside the seas. The beaches grew higher and higher, until they were mounds, then hills, then great mountains, and until, at last, they became enormous barriers that stood against the raging waters.

When the waters saw the great army of mountains created by the tiny grains of sand, and saw how courageously the grains stood united, they became frightened, and retreated.

Thus, as the waters came to respect the tiny grains of sand and their strength when joined together, they learned to live in harmony with the other creations of the earth.

Gimel ג, the third letter of the alphabet, is related to gamol, which means to nourish until completely ripe, or bring to maturity, like a child's growth. Gimel has a value of three and is a symbol of kindness and culmination.

Morning Star

Once upon a time, long ago, before the great floods covered the earth, lived a beautiful young girl named Istahar. At the end of each day, when the sun set and the stars began to rise, she would go outside, sit under her favorite tree, and watch the heavens. As the moon and stars moved across the great sky, wonder filled her heart.

Sometimes falling stars flashed across the night sky. She would follow each one as far as her eyes allowed, then tried to imagine where it had gone. "Oh, how I wish I could find a star of my own," she thought. God heard her wish.

One night a huge star shot across the sky. She watched it as she always did, but this shooting star was different. It did not disappear. Instead, it stopped and grew brighter and brighter. It grew so bright that she could no longer look at it directly. Then, amazingly, the star came toward her, lighting up everything around her. As a gust of wind blew across her face, Istahar saw a dazzling light on a tree branch above her, looking like a full moon. She gasped, "Could my dreams have come true? Could this be a falling star of my very own?"

Istahar wanted to get closer to the glowing ball of light, so she climbed up the tree and onto the branch on which it was perched. As she got closer, she discovered that it was surprisingly cool. It was so cool that she could actually touch it. She reached for the light, closed her hand around it, and cautiously came down again.

Once she was back on the ground, she carefully examined the ball. "If this is not a star, what is it?" she wondered. The light was glowing, like an immense jewel

that sparkled with multicolored lights radiating from within. Deep down she saw a burning flame, and in the center of the flame she saw a face.

The longer she looked at the face, the clearer it became. From a distance Istahar heard a strong and gentle voice. "Dear child, I am the angel Raziel. In your hand you hold a magic jewel that has fallen from the Throne of Glory. This jewel must be returned to God's Home and put back in its proper place. If it is not returned, the people of the earth will miss a great blessing from God."

"How can I help?" asked Istahar.

"You yourself must return the jewel to God's Throne. Someone will come to you and ask for the jewel. He who comes may be a demon or an angel. You must not give up the jewel to either one of them. Even the angel will not return the jewel to its proper place; only you can accomplish this task. The others are tempted by the power of the precious treasure."

"A demon! An angel trying to steal God's jewel! Oh, dear! I can't do this. I'm only a little girl. I won't know what to say, or what to do!"

"I will give you instructions," said Raziel. "If he who comes to you does not cast a shadow, then a demon stands before you. If he who comes has wings, you have an angel in your midst. When you ask the demon why there are no shadows around him, he will disappear immediately. If it is an angel who stands before you, you must find a way to get his wings. As soon as you have the wings on, hold the jewel tightly in your hands, and you will know what to do. Everything now depends on you." The angel in the flame vanished, and the flame dimmed until it was gone.

The moon slipped behind a cloud, and the night

Source ~ "Morning Star" is a fairy tale from thirteenth-century Germany.

In an early version, Istahar escapes the angel by insisting that he reveal to her the secret Name of God. After the angel tells her the Name, she pronounces it, flies into heaven, and is rewarded by God who transforms her into a star.

grew darker. The girl heard another voice, "You can see that the jewel is useless now. It has grown dark inside and out. Why don't you just toss it away." Frightened, Istahar started to pray.

The dark cloud slowly passed and the full moon once again shone bright. Istahar then became aware of a dark figure standing beside her, and noticed that the figure cast no shadow. She then remembered what the angel had told her, and some of her fear melted away. "This must be the demon that wants to steal the jewel," she thought.

"I see that you do not have a shadow!" she said, trying to sound very bold. To her surprise, the demon vanished immediately.

Istahar now noticed that the flame had returned to the jewel. In the distance, she saw a tiny light. It grew brighter as it became closer and closer, until it was right beside her. Its glow was so brilliant that she had to cover her eyes. Her fear returned. She could barely speak when she asked, "Who are you?"

"I am an angel who has been sent to recover the fallen jewel," said the glowing figure. The angel's shimmering wings beat back and forth.

"I believe you, " said Istahar. "I will give you the jewel, if you grant me one favor first. I wish to try on your wings."

"I can't let you try my wings on. They do not come off."

"If you are a real angel, anything is possible. Surely this is a very tiny request. Maybe you are not a real angel!"

"Of course I'm a real angel, and I can do anything. I'll show you." the angel said. He removed his magnificent wings and handed them to Istahar.

She put the wings on and felt their power as they beat back and forth. Instantly, she knew how she would return the precious jewel to its proper place. She made a small jump up, and away she flew. She flew upward, upward as the helpless angel watched from the ground.

Past the moon, through the stars, she soared, winging her way to heaven. When she stopped, she was standing before the Throne of Glory. She counted nine glowing jewels around the Throne, and a tenth space that was empty. The inner flame of the jewel began to glow brighter and brighter. Istahar placed the precious jewel in its space on the Throne of Glory.

At that moment, all the angels in heaven rejoiced and sang the most beautiful music ever heard. The voices of the angels rose in joy to praise her. She then heard another voice, a voice that seemed to speak from inside and outside of her at the same time. She knew this to be the voice of God.

"My dearest child, because of your courage and brave deed, the world will receive a great blessing. I will make you the morning star, the brightest star in all the sky."

On her cheek Istahar felt a gentle kiss. She felt herself grow bright. The darkness around her filled with light. And from that day forth, people on earth have looked into the sky and blessed the morning star, the one that shines brighter than all the rest.

The planet Venus, the brightest object in the sky, is called the morning star when it appears in the east at sunrise, and the evening star when it is in the west at sunset.

Dalet ד, the fourth letter of the alphabet, has a value of four, and is the symbol of the dimensions of the physical world that extend in the four directions — north, south, east, and west.

The Princess of
the Third Pumpkin

Once upon a time, in the land of Israel, lived a king and queen with their only child, a son. When the prince became of age they told him that the time had come for him to choose a bride and marry. The son agreed that he would gladly marry if he could find the right bride. The king sent for the most beautiful maidens in all the land to come before the prince. Maidens came from far and wide, but the prince was not pleased by any of them. Then the king sent out another proclamation promising that whoever brought the right bride to his son would be richly rewarded.

One day an old woman arrived at the palace and asked to be presented to the king. When she was brought to him the old woman said, "Lord king, I have a maiden for the prince who is unique in all the world."

"Where is this special maiden?" asked the king. "Bring her to me!"

"The prince must rise at dawn and go into the palace garden," replied the old woman. "He must put on his coat and take with him a bottle of water and a knife. In the garden he will find three pumpkins growing on a single vine. With his knife he is to cut off one of the pumpkins, and from this pumpkin will emerge the most beautiful princess in the whole world. If he gives her a drink of water, she will desire to be his bride."

The king thanked the old woman, and told his courier to take her to a small hut in the courtyard behind the royal kitchen and to provide for all her needs. The king then called for his son and told him how to find the pumpkin princess.

The prince did exactly as his father had instructed. He rose at dawn the next morning, put on his coat, and went into the royal garden with a knife and a bottle of water. Sure enough, he found three pumpkins growing on a single vine. He carefully cut one of the pumpkins off the vine, and instantly a beautiful princess appeared. "A drink, a drink, please, quickly!" she cried. But before the prince could get the bottle of water to her lips, she vanished from sight. The prince cut another pumpkin from the vine, and another beautiful princess appeared. She also cried out, "Oh, a drink, a drink, please!" But before the prince could give her the water, she too vanished. The prince cut the third pumpkin from the vine, and a princess as beautiful as a sunrise stepped forth. She cried, "A drink, a drink, a drink!" This time the prince

Source ~ "The Princess of the Third Pumpkin" is a folktale from nine-teenth-century Russia.

The folktale, märchen in Yiddish, is said to be the crown of folk culture.

quickly put the bottle to her lips. She drank and drank, until the water was gone. The prince took off his coat, wrapped it around the princess, and placed her on a branch of a tree beside a well. He kissed her gently on the cheek and told her to wait for his return. Then the prince hurried off to tell his father and mother that he had found the bride of his dreams.

While the prince was gone, an old gypsy woman wandered into the garden and stopped at the well for water. As she reached into the well, she saw the reflection of the princess. Thinking it was her own reflection, she exclaimed, "Oh my, how beautiful I am!"

The princess heard her and said, "You silly old gypsy! You don't see yourself. You see me. I am the one who is beautiful, the one the prince will marry."

Startled, the gypsy looked up at the tree and saw the beautiful princess. She snatched her from the tree, pulled off the prince's coat, and threw the princess into the well. As soon as the princess touched the water, she turned into a golden fish. The gypsy put on the prince's coat, climbed onto the tree branch, and waited for the prince to return. She then cast a magic spell that would make the prince see the pumpkin princess whenever he looked at the gypsy.

The joyful king and queen entered the garden in order to see the beautiful princess who had won the heart of their beloved son. When they looked up in the tree and saw the old gypsy, they gasped and wondered why their son would want this gypsy for a bride. But, wanting only happiness for their beloved son, they said nothing to him about his strange choice. The queen sent beautiful clothes for the gypsy, and the king escorted her to the palace. Soon the entire palace was busy with preparations for the wedding banquet.

When the king's cook went to the well to draw water, he found the golden fish swimming in the bottom of his pail. "This fish will be perfect for the royal banquet," he thought. So he took the beautiful fish to the kitchen, cooked it, and threw the fish scales into the garden. When the old woman who lived beside the royal kitchen saw the golden fish scales, she gathered the scales up into her apron and took them back to her little hut. She sewed them together to make a tablecloth for the banquet table. She wove the cloth in the design of the royal garden with a portrait of the pumpkin princess in its center. She then entered the palace and presented the tablecloth to the king and queen.

They were so delighted with the tablecloth's exquisite design and beauty that they had it placed on the banquet table for the prince and his bride. As the guests were enjoying the banquet feast, the prince noticed the tablecloth. "Who wove this tablecloth?" he gasped. He was so struck by the princess's portrait.

"The old woman who lives in the hut near the kitchen made the tablecloth," answered the king.

The prince commanded that the old woman be brought to him at once. When she arrived the prince asked, "Was it you who wove this tablecloth?"

"Yes, Sire," replied the old woman, "it is a portrait of the true pumpkin princess who was turned into a golden fish."

The prince ordered the old woman to make the princess appear. When the prince saw the pumpkin princess he recognized her as his true beloved. He wept for joy, embraced her, and kissed her. As he did so, the spell of the gypsy bride was broken, and she was driven from the palace forever. The prince and princess were married and continue to live happily to this very day.

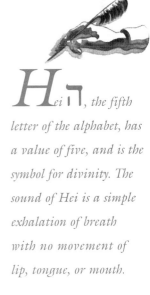

Hei ה, the fifth letter of the alphabet, has a value of five, and is the symbol for divinity. The sound of Hei is a simple exhalation of breath with no movement of lip, tongue, or mouth.

The Old Crone and the Little Girl

Once upon a time, long, long ago, a very old crone lived in a tiny hut in the forest. She was known far and wide as one who taught naughty children how to be good.

Now, it happened that one day a mother came to the old crone with her young daughter. "My daughter will not listen to me and refuses to do what I ask of her. Here, you take her, and teach her how to behave so that we can live in peace."

The old crone walked slowly around the little girl; she looked her up and down and all around, and replied, "Yes, I can do that. Leave her with me." And that is how the little girl came to live with the old crone.

One day the old crone took the little girl into the forest to gather some kindling for the stove. While they were gone a big brown bear came to the hut. He began to dance and twirl around and around. He was having a very fine time. Then a beautiful stag came along. He looked questioningly at the twirling bear and said, "What are you doing dancing around like that?"

The bear didn't stop, but said, "What difference does it make? I'm having fun. Why don't you join me and dance also?"

"All right, I will join you." answered the stag.

And the bear and the stag twirled around and around.

Source ~"The Old Crone and the Little Girl" is a folktale from nineteenth-century Romania.

The Old Crone is similar in character to Baba Yaga, the best-known witch in Russian folklore.

While they were dancing, a dog came by and asked, "Hey, bear! Hey, stag! Why are you dancing like that?"

"What difference does it make?" replied the bear and the stag. "Why don't you join us and dance along?" The dog jumped right in, and soon all three of them were twirling about. A rooster strolled by. When he saw the three dancing, he stopped and asked, "Why are you all twirling around like that?"

"What difference does it make?" replied the bear, the stag, and the dog, "Why don't you join us and dance too?" And now all four were dancing and laughing and having a good time. They twirled and twirled as fast as they could.

Next, a teapot came along. It stopped and asked, "Bear, dog, stag, and rooster, why are you dancing like this?"

"What difference does it make?" they all answered breathlessly. "Why don't you join us and dance too?" Now all five were spinning around and around. Soon a bit of tar and a sharp pin came walking by. They stopped and asked, "What are all of you doing twirling around like that?"

"What difference does it make?" each answered, "You could join us and dance too." Then all seven danced and twirled and had a wonderful time. As nighttime came upon them, they became hungry for dinner and ready for sleep.

The stag asked, "Where shall we find food for dinner?"

"And where can we find a nice warm place to sleep?" asked the rooster.

The bear looked around and said, "Here, inside the old crone's hut, we'll find everything we need." The bear led the way and the others followed him into the tiny hut. And sure enough, they found all the food they wanted, plus warm and cozy places to sleep.

The bear got into the old crone's bed, the dog jumped into the cradle, and the stag found a place behind the stove. The rooster perched on a high shelf, the teapot crawled up the chimney, the bit of tar got inside a box of matches, and the pin stuck itself into a soft hand towel. Each was soon fast asleep.

When the old crone and the little girl returned, they put the bundles of kindling down and, tired from the day's work, went into the hut to sleep. When they crawled into bed, the bear rolled over and knocked them to the floor. Frightened, the old crone motioned to the girl to follow. She whispered, "Hide in the cradle." When they climbed into the cradle, they disturbed the dog, which bit the crone. "Ouch," she cried, "What is happening here?"

When she ran to hide behind the stove, she fell onto the stag's huge, sharp horns, and turned cold with fear. She leaned into the fireplace to get warm, but the teapot fell out of the chimney and onto her head. Shaking, and rubbing the bump on her head, she called out, "Oh, woe is me! What's going on here?" She grabbed her lamp and reached into the matchbox for a match, but the bit of tar stuck to her fingers and she couldn't shake it off. So she tried to wash the tar off her fingers and when she grabbed the hand towel, the pin pricked her finger and she screamed out in pain. The rooster heard her and yelled back, "You don't scare me!"

The old crone was so frightened that she dropped to the floor and died, right there on the spot!

The little girl saw that this was her chance to escape. She ran out of the hut and kept on running until she got all the way home. She fell into her mother's arms and, from that day on, she never again disobeyed her parents. And that is why, to this very day, children everywhere listen to their parents, and try to do what is asked of them.

Vav ‎ו, *the sixth letter of the alphabet, has a value of six, and symbolizes completion. In the physical world a complete self-contained object consists of six dimensions: above and below, right and left, before and behind.*

The Lost Princess

Once upon a time there was a king who had six sons whom he loved dearly. But his favorite child was his daughter, a young princess who was known for her stubbornness. This upset and angered the king. Once, when the princess refused to obey the king's wishes, he became so angry that he lost his temper. He screamed a curse at her. "Be gone with you! May the Devil take you!"

The young princess gathered her long skirts up in her arms and ran from the king's chamber. The king soon

realized he had done a terrible thing. The next morning he went to the princess's room to apologize. The princess was gone. The king's servants searched and searched, but the princess was nowhere to be found.

The sorrowful king grieved for his lost daughter. He finally called in his most trusted viceroy, and instructed him to search the world, and to not return until he had found the princess.

The viceroy and his servant wandered the earth for a long time. One day they came to a path that led into a dark forest. Hoping it would lead to the princess, the viceroy decided to turn off the main road and travel that path. They stayed on this path until they came to a large fortress guarded by soldiers. Leaving his servant behind, the viceroy entered the fortress alone. To his great surprise, the guards let him pass without hesitation. Once inside the fortress, he went from room to room until he came to a large hall. At the end of the hall, a king with a magnificent crown upon his head sat on a throne. Soldiers lined the walls of the long hall, and musicians played while ladies danced and threw flowers before the king. Banquet tables were covered with exotic delicacies. No one seemed to notice the viceroy as he stood quietly by in the corner.

Then trumpets sounded as ladies in waiting ushered in the beautiful queen. All in her path bowed low as she passed. When she took her seat beside the king, the viceroy saw her face. He recognized her as the lost princess! And the queen recognized the viceroy. She rose from her throne and came to him. Touching his arm gently, she asked, "Do you know who I am?"

"You are the lost princess," he answered. "How does it happen that you are here?"

"My father's curse sent me here," answered the

Source ~ "The Lost Princess" is a fairy tale dating from early nineteenth-century Poland.

princess. "You do not recognize it, but this is the kingdom of the Evil One."

The viceroy told the princess that for many years he has been searching for her, at her father's request. He also told her how much her father longed for her, how much he loved her, and how ashamed he was of his actions. "Is there a way for me to rescue you from this place?" asked the viceroy.

"There is only one way," she said. "You must spend a whole year in one place, and every day you must yearn with all your heart to free me. On the last day of the year you may neither eat nor sleep."

The viceroy did as he was told until the last day of his year. On that day, he tried to neither eat nor sleep, but he came upon an apple tree filled with the most delicious-looking apples he had ever seen. He felt such a strong craving for an apple that he climbed the tree, picked one, and ate it. He then fell into a deep, deep sleep from which his servant could not wake him. And so he slept for a long time.

The viceroy awoke feeling sorrowful. He had failed to rescue the princess. He returned to the fortress and found that the princess was still there.

"You have lost your chance to free me," said the princess. "If you had come at the right time, I would have been freed. I know that staying awake is very difficult, especially on the last day, but that is what you must do. Go to another place and spend one year in the same way. Remember, on the last day you must not sleep. And do not eat or drink anything. Wakefulness is everything!"

Again the viceroy did as he was told. Yet, on the last day of the year, he stopped beside a bubbling spring that was red and fragrant, like wine. "Have you ever seen

anything like this?" he asked his servant. "It should be water, yet it is red and smells like wine."

He knelt before the stream, sipped a handful of the cool liquid and immediately fell fast asleep for many years. While he slept, the princess came by in her carriage. "How long and how many trials will it take before he frees me? One day it will be too late." She took a veil from her head and on it she wrote a message with her tears. She then placed it on the ground beside the viceroy.

When the viceroy awoke, his servant told him about the wine, and about the princess and how she had cried. "What is this?" he asked his servant when he saw the veil. After his servant explained how the princess had written on it with her tears, the viceroy held the veil up to the sunlight, and the secret message became clear. It said that she soon would be taken from the fortress and moved to the castle of diamonds on the the mountain of gold.

The viceroy now set out alone to search for the princess. After having traveled through all the civilized lands of the world, he now found himself in the wilderness. One day he came upon a giant who was carrying an enormous tree on his shoulders.

"Who are you?" the giant asked the viceroy.

"I am a man."

"No men come into this wilderness," said the giant. "I have lived here for many years and have never seen a man."

The viceroy explained to the giant that he was looking for a castle of diamonds on a mountain of gold.

"Oh no," said the giant, "I assure you there's no such thing here!"

Distraught, the viceroy collapsed and started to cry. The giant took pity on the man and said, "There is one

This tale is attributed to Rabbi Nachman of Bratslav, a tzaddik who was born in 1772. He was the great-grandson of the Baal Shem Tov, and was well known as a traveling wonder-worker. A devoted group of Hasidim follow his teachings to this day.

thing that I can do for you that may give you some peace of mind. I'm in charge of the beasts. I'll summon them and you can ask if they know of this castle and mountain." The giant then summoned all of the beasts, from the smallest to the largest, and asked them if they knew of the castle or the mountain. The beasts all said that they had never seen or heard of them.

"See," said the giant to the viceroy, "What you are trying to find doesn't exist. Go back!"

But the viceroy would not give up. He insisted that the mountain and castle must be somewhere. The giant scratched his huge chin. "There is one more thing we can try. My brother lives in this wilderness. He's in charge of all the birds. Perhaps the high-soaring birds have seen what you are looking for. Go to my brother. Tell him I sent you."

The viceroy traveled on until he came upon another giant carrying another large tree. The viceroy told him that he was sent by his brother, and pleaded with him to summon the birds. The giant called forth all the birds, from the smallest to the largest, and asked them if they knew of the castle of diamonds or the mountain of gold. None of the birds had ever seen or heard of them. "Go back to where you came from and forget this foolish quest," the giant told the viceroy.

But the viceroy would not give up. Finally, the second giant said, "There is one more brother in the wilderness who may be able to help you. He's in charge of the winds."

So the viceroy journeyed until he found another giant carrying a huge tree on his shoulders. This giant also said that he knew nothing of the castle and the mountain, but he did agree to call the winds. When the winds had gathered, the giant asked them about the castle of

diamonds and the mountain of gold. The winds said they had never seen or heard of them. "You see," said the giant, "Just as I told you, there's no such thing!"

The viceroy fell to the ground in tears and cried out, "It must exist!"

Just then, one last wind arrived. "What made you late?" scolded the giant. "Why didn't you come on time like the others?"

"I was late because I was bringing a princess to a castle of diamonds on a mountain of gold."

"What?" screamed the viceroy, jumping up with joy.

The giant said to the wind, "What will this man need to get to the mountain and into the castle"

"The man must pay with gold," replied the wind.

Then the giant handed a golden bowl to the viceroy. "Because you have searched for such a long time, and have gone through so much to find the princess, I'm giving you this magic bowl. Whenever you put your hand in it, you will be able to take out as much gold as will be needed to pay for her rescue."

The giant told the wind to take the viceroy to the mountain. So the whirling wind carried him to the mountain of gold and set him down before the city's gates. The soldiers guarding the gates refused to let the viceroy enter until he had paid them. The viceroy put his hand into the bowl and pulled out the amount of gold demanded by the guards. Once inside the city, he made his way to the castle of diamonds and found the princess.

How did he get her out? That he did not tell. But he did return her safely to her father's palace. The king honored the viceroy with a great feast. Soon thereafter, the viceroy asked the princess to be his bride. All the people of the kingdom joined their king in the joyous wedding celebration of the viceroy and the princess.

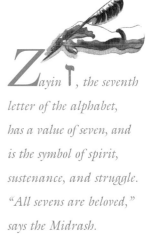

Zayin ז, the seventh letter of the alphabet, has a value of seven, and is the symbol of spirit, sustenance, and struggle. "All sevens are beloved," says the Midrash.

69

A Present for a Princess

Once upon a time, in the land of Israel, there lived a beautiful princess who loved three handsome brothers. When the time came for the princess to marry, it was hard for her to choose among them. Since each of the brothers was in love with the princess and wanted to be chosen as her prince, she decreed a marriage test. Each brother was to comb the world for the most precious object he could find. Whoever returned with the object that she valued most, would become her prince. The brothers agreed to show one another the objects they had found before presenting them to the princess.

And so each brother set out on his quest. The oldest brother went to China, where he visited many strange and exotic cities. In the markets and bazaars he found exquisite silks and rich tapestries, but nothing wonderful enough for the princess. Then, one day, an old man showed him a magic carpet, a carpet that would transport him to any place he wanted to go. He was thrilled! He paid the old man for the carpet, sat upon it, and flew to his home, feeling certain he had the gift that would win the heart of the princess.

In the meantime, the middle brother was in the land of Egypt. He met a magician there who told him about the many wonders to be found in that mysterious place, and promised to show him the greatest wonder of all. He then held up a shining piece of glass. "But this is just a simple mirror," said the brother.

Source ~ "A Present for a Princess" is a fairy tale from ancient Palestine.

"Oh no, this is no ordinary mirror. Whenever you wish to see a place – any place, all you have to do is think about it. You will see it right here, in this mirror!" The brother looked in the mirror and thought of his home. Sure enough, just as the magician had said, there it was! He could see his older brother waiting for him. He gladly paid the magician, and set off for home, confident that his gift would win the heart of the princess.

Now, the youngest brother was in the ancient land of Arabia. Magical fruit grew here that could make one tall, or strong, or very rich. One day, the brother came upon a farmer tilling an orchard. He told him about the princess and about his quest for a precious gift.

"Kind Sir," said the farmer, "come with me. I have something I think will be of great interest to you." The farmer led the brother far into the orchard to a clearing. He tapped three times on a stone, and a beautiful apple tree rose out of the ground. The farmer picked a single apple and handed it to the young man. "This tree grew in the Garden of Eden, and this apple is forever ripe. It will cure any illness or heal any pain, but its magic will work only once." The brother gave the farmer all the money he had and set off for home with the apple safely tucked away in his traveling bag. He hoped with all his might that his object would win the princess.

When the brothers were reunited at their home, they spoke of their adventures and shared with one another the treasures they had found. The youngest brother suggested that they try out the magic mirror and look for the princess. When they looked in the mirror they were shocked to see the princess lying in her bed, looking pale and thin and gasping for breath. A team of doctors surrounded her, pacing back and forth. The brothers could see that the princess was dying.

The oldest brother pulled his siblings onto the magic carpet. They flew across the kingdom to the palace, and dashed to the bedside of the princess. The youngest brother took the magic apple from his bag and gently held her head up, saying, "Here, this will make you well." As soon as the princess bit into the apple the magic in it began to heal her. Color returned to her cheeks, she breathed more easily, and her temperature started to come down. Her family, her doctors, and the three brothers all gave thanks to God.

Once the princess was completely well, she summoned the brothers to the palace. The oldest brother told her of the magic carpet that enabled them to reach her bedside in time. He said he hoped she would choose this as the most precious object. The second brother said his magic mirror was more precious because through it they had been able to see that she was dying. The youngest brother told her about the apple and how he had used its power to heal her. The oldest brother then asked the princess whose hand she would accept in marriage.

The princess said she loved each brother, but could marry only one. She embraced the eldest brother and thanked him for the magic carpet. She embraced the second brother and thanked him for the magic mirror. She then stretched out her hand to the youngest brother and said, "I have chosen you to be my husband. The magic mirror can be used many times, the carpet will fly for anyone, but the magic in the apple could be used only once. You could have saved it for yourself, but you gave it to me." The princess kissed the handsome youth, and a joyful wedding celebration took place that very night.

The use of the magic carpet speaks of the tale's Middle Eastern origin.

73

One Only Kid – Had Gadya

One only kid, only one kid, which my father bought for two Zuzim.

One only kid, only one kid.

Then came the cat and ate the kid, which my father bought for two Zuzim.

One only kid, only one kid.

Then came the dog and bit the cat that ate the kid, which my father bought for two Zuzim.

One only kid, only one kid.

Then came the stick and beat the dog that bit the cat, which my father bought for two Zuzim.

One only kid, only one kid.

Then came the fire and burned the stick that beat the dog that bit the cat that ate the kid, which my father bought for two Zuzim.

One only kid, only one kid.

Source ~ "One Only Kid – Had Gadya," is an Aramaic nursery song, or rhyme, of unknown origin, but traced back as far as the ninth century.

In this nursery song kid means young goat.

Then came the waters that quenched the fire that burned the stick that beat the dog that bit the cat that ate the kid, which my father bought for two Zuzim.

One only kid, only one kid.

Then came the ox and drank the waters that quenched the fire that burned the stick that beat the dog that bit the cat that ate the kid, which my father bought for two Zuzim.

One only kid, only one kid.

Then came the slaughterer and killed the ox that drank the waters that quenched the fire that burned the stick that beat the dog that bit the cat that ate the kid, which my father bought for two Zuzim.

One only kid, only one kid.

Then came the Angel of Death and slew the slaughterer that killed the ox that drank the waters that quenched the fire that burned the stick that beat the dog that bit the cat that ate the kid, which my father bought for two Zuzim.

One only kid, only one kid.

Then came the Most Holy, praised be He, and removed the Angel of Death that slew the slaughterer that killed the ox that drank the waters that quenched the fire that burned the stick that beat the dog that bit the cat that ate the kid, which my father bought for two Zuzim.

One only kid, only one kid.

Abram, look to the east, look to the west, look to the north, and look to the south. All the land that you see I give to you and your children forever. Rise and walk the distance of this land for it belongs to you.

— "The Story of Abraham"

First to Third Grades

The First Day of Creation

God created the heavens from the Light of His garment. He took His garment and stretched it out and the heavens extended farther and farther, until He cried out to them to stop. "Be stayed," He said, "it is far enough." And they stopped. And then the Creator took the snow from beneath His Throne of Glory and scattered it upon the waters. And the waters became liquid, and the earth became snow. The poles of the heavens He fixed in the waters of the ocean that flow between the ends of the heavens and the ends of the earth. He created the four corners of the world — east, south, west, and north. From the corner facing east there goes forth into the world light and heat. The corner facing south sends forth blessings of dew and rain. The treasures of snow and hail are stored in the corner facing west. From there, cold descends upon the world. But the corner facing north was not completed. This corner is the home of lightning and thunder, of winds and of earthquakes. Here also dwell the demons and spirits. It is from this corner that evil breaks forth and comes upon the world. The Creator said, "Let anyone come and finish this corner, and then the world will know that he is a God."

Source ~ "The First Day of Creation" is a post-biblical aggadah on the creation story found in Genesis.

The Hebrew calendar, which is based on the phases of the moon, begins at the traditional date of the creation of the universe. The year 2000 will be 5760-61 in the Hebrew calendar.

Chet ח, *the eighth letter of the alphabet, has a value of eight, and symbolizes all that exists on the plane above nature that is divine or metaphysical.*

Stone Birds

Long, long ago King Solomon was known far and wide as the wisest of humankind. His great wisdom allowed him to know the languages of all the birds in the air and all the beasts on the ground. He could speak to the animals in the forests, the fowl in the barnyard, and even to the fish in the sea. One day, as he sat in his palace garden on the Temple Mount enjoying the bright

*S*ource ~ "Stone Birds" is one of the King Solomon legends dating from fifth-century Babylonia.

King Solomon, who was the builder of the Great Temple, Beit Hamikdash, reigned in ancient Israel from 961-922 B.C.E.

Revered as one of the wisest sages in Biblical history, Solomon is credited with writing 3000 proverbs and 1005 songs.

— 1 KINGS 4:32

sunlight and cool breezes, he noticed two cooing birds in the tree above him. The birds twittered merrily as they caressed one another.

Solomon heard the male bird ask his mate, "Who is that man seated there?"

"That is King Solomon. He is the mightiest and wisest king in all the lands."

"Why do you call him mighty?" mocked her mate. "Is he really powerful enough to have so many palaces and fortresses at his command? If I so desired I could overthrow him in a second, just by fluttering one wing."

The bird was impressed and encouraged her mate by saying, "Then do so, and show your might and power. See if you have the strength to carry out your words."

King Solomon, who was listening to the birds' conversation, called to the male bird to join him on the garden bench. The bird trembled slightly, but flew down to sit beside Solomon. The great King asked the bird how he came to have such overwhelming pride.

The bird answered, "My Lord, out of your loving kindness and goodness of heart, please grant me forgiveness. I am but a poor, powerless bird that can do no evil. What I said was intended only to please my mate and impress her with my own greatness." King Solomon smiled to himself and sent the bird back to his mate.

Meanwhile, the bird's mate perched high in a tree and waited anxiously for him to return. When he came back she asked excitedly, "Quickly, tell me, why did the King send for you? What did he say?"

"King Solomon heard my words," answered the bird, his chest swelling with pride, "and he begged me not to carry out my plan of overthrowing him because it would bring destruction to his court."

"This is something I would like to see," said the female bird. "Show me your strength, and then we'll see what happens to Solomon's great court."

When Solomon heard the false tale of the brazen bird and the reckless encouragement of his mate, he grew very angry. When he had finally heard enough he decided to change both birds into stone statues. He wanted them to remain forever as a warning to others not to engage in vain bragging and empty boasting, and to teach them that it is dangerous to incite others to do foolish and mindless deeds.

The stone birds still stand today at the southern wall of the Mosque of Omar, which is on the site of King Solomon's Temple.

The Mosque of Omar is on the site of King Solomon's Temple in Jerusalem's old city. Red veins running through a slab with a black border show the outlines of the two birds that Solomon turned to stone.

The Witches of Ashkelon

Long, long ago, in a cave on the outskirts of the city of Ashkelon, there lived a coven of eighty witches. These witches had been tormenting the good people of Ashkelon for hundreds of years. Some of the witches cast spells that were merely annoying, such as extinguishing home fires, or turning wine into vinegar. Others used their witchcraft to cause great hardships. They destroyed Ashkelon's food supply by casting spells on the cows, so there would be no milk, or by ruining the crops with great floods or long droughts. Some of the witches preferred to direct their evil at just one person, or just one family, such as the time they came to the home of one of the town's rabbis.

The witches burst into the rabbi's house while he was at supper with his wife and children. The witches waved their magic wands and turned the rabbi into a bird. They then waved their magic wands again and turned his wife into a butterfly. The children watched helplessly as the bird and butterfly flew out the window.

News of this tragic event spread quickly through the town. The people of Ashkelon were outraged and, once again, they appealed to the town's eldest rabbi for help. Once and for all, they wanted to rid their town of the terrible curse of the evil witches.

Source ~ "The Witches of Ashkelon" is an aggadah legend found in the Jerusalem Talmud

---

Another famous biblical sorceress, the Witch of Endor, was known to summon spirits and wizards.
— 1 SAMUEL 28:7

The eldest rabbi had vowed to God to help the people of Ashkelon. But because of the power of evil the witches had at their command, the rabbi had hesitated to take action against them. Then one of his disciples came to tell him that he had had a dream, a dream that caused the rabbi to change his mind.

In the dream, the disciple was walking beside a river near a forest. He saw the rabbi on the other side of the river trying to get across the water. Miriam, the sister of Moses, suddenly appeared at the disciple's side with an iron key in her hand. The disciple asked her what the key was for. "This is the key to the gates of Hell where the souls of the wicked are punished. I've come to deliver the key to your master because he has not fulfilled his vow to God to rid Ashkelon of the curse of the witches."

When the disciple awoke he hurried to the old rabbi and told him of his dream. "Because I have told no one about my vow to help the people of Ashkelon eliminate the witches," said the rabbi, "I have no doubt that this dream is a message to me from Heaven."

So, without a moment's delay, the rabbi went to work on a plan to do away with the witches. As soon as the rainy season came, he called together eighty townsmen to help him carry out his plan. He told each man to bring a long robe, folded and placed in a large pot, to a meeting place at the edge of town. When all the men were gathered, he told them to place the pots upside down on top of their heads. He then led the men along a path until they came to a cave that was directly next to the witches' cave. He entered this cave with the men, asked them to wait, and gave them these instructions: "When you hear me whistle once, put on your long robes; when you hear me whistle the second time, join together and enter the witches' cave. Once

you have entered their cave, each one of you must take hold of a witch and dance with her; as you are dancing you must twirl the witch off the ground. Once you have a witch in the air, do not allow her feet to touch the ground, for as we know, when a witch's feet leave the earth, she is completely powerless."

The rabbi was now ready to visit the witches' cave. He walked the short distance through heavy rain. When he arrived at their cave door he slipped into his dry robe and knocked three times. From inside a witch called out, "Who is there?"

"I am one of your own!" replied the rabbi.

"What do you want?" screeched the witch.

"I am a sorcerer and I want to show you my powers…and I want to see your powers."

"Powers? What powers do you have that you think would be of interest to us?" said another witch as the others started to gather around.

"I can make appear before you eighty men in long robes who will want to dance with you," answered the rabbi.

When the witches heard this they cackled and rubbed their bony hands together in excitement. "Do come in," said the leader of the coven, "This is indeed a feat we would like to see you perform."

When the rabbi stepped into the witches' cave they saw at once that his robe was dry. Curious, they gathered close to him. One witch asked, "How can your robe remain dry in such a storm as we have tonight?"

"I make myself so tiny that I can walk between the raindrops."

The witches jumped back and gasped. "How is it that you have these great powers?" asked the leader of the coven.

The city of Ashkelon, which dates from Biblical times, is near the coast of the Mediterranean Sea, about forty miles southwest of Jerusalem.

"I will show you in time," replied the rabbi cautiously, "but first I must see some of the powers you possess."

The witches were delighted to show off their powers to such a talented visitor. The first witch made a table move to the center of the room just by raising her hand. Another made a tablecloth appear out of thin air. A third witch conjured up an incredible feast of the finest food and drink. Then the leader of the coven stepped forward and said, "That's enough! Now it is your turn to show us what you can do." And all the witches formed a circle around the rabbi.

"Very well, I will now show you the wonders I promised," said the rabbi. "After I have whistled twice, eighty men will appear. Each man will be as dry as I am, and each will want to dance with one of you." The rabbi whistled once. The men heard the whistle and put on their dry robes. The witches were all atwitter. When he whistled the second time, they entered the witches' cave. The witches laughed excitedly when the men appeared. As the "sorcerer" had promised, the robes of the men were dry, and each man asked a witch to dance. The witches jumped into the men's arms and soon were whirling around the room. As they danced and twirled, the men lifted the witches off the ground. At first the witches thought it was a part of the dance and shrieked with delight, but when the men started to carry them outside and into the rain, they began to kick and scream.

The witches were terrified of rain. They knew that as soon as the water touched them they would be transformed, and all of the spells they had cast would be broken forever. And this is exactly what happened to the witches of Ashkelon when the townsmen danced the witches into the rain.

The witches who had stopped the rain from falling were turned into puddles, the puddles formed a stream that flowed into a river, and the river ran into the sea becoming seawater. The seawater evaporated and rose up into the sky and formed clouds. In time these clouds grew full and the water fell back down to earth as rain. The witches who had extinguished the hearth fires burst into flames and burned until only their ashes remained. The ashes were scattered in the fields and absorbed by the soil. Soon the soil was again fertile. The witches who had changed wine into vinegar were changed into grapes hanging on a vine; the grapes were later picked, crushed in the winepress, and made into wine. The witches who had caused the milk to dry up were turned into green grass for the pasture where the cows grazed, and soon the cows of Ashkelon were once again producing milk. Finally, the witches who had turned the rabbi and his wife into a bird and a butterfly were turned into worms; the worms scurried along the ground and were soon swallowed by hungry birds.

When all the witches were transformed, and all of the spells they had cast were broken, the bird and the butterfly turned back into the rabbi and his wife and returned home to their children. Thus, all the witches were punished for their evil deeds, and the city of Ashkelon was free of their curse for all time.

Tet ט, the ninth letter of the alphabet, has a value of nine, and is the symbol of goodness. The Hebrew word for good is "tov." Moses was called Tovia because he was so good.

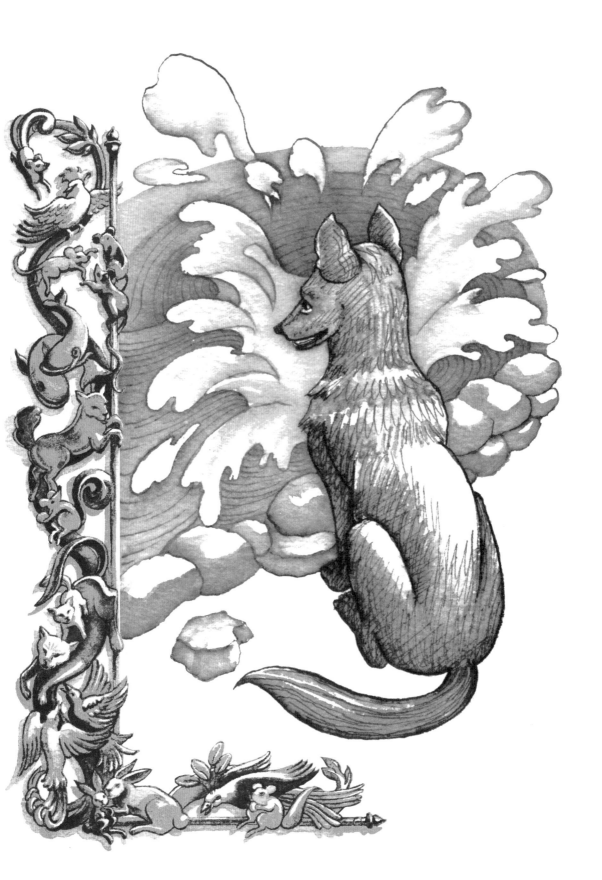

The Dog's Reflection

Once upon a time there was a dog that took a hunk of meat from a family table and carried it away in his mouth. He thought about the delicious feast he would have when he got home. His path took him deep into the woods, turning this way and that, until he came to a bridge. As he crossed the bridge, he happened to glance down into the water, and saw the reflection of the meat in his mouth. The dog thought, "I could have a really big feast tonight if I also had the meat that is down there in the water. Two pieces of meat are certainly better than one." The dog walked on but couldn't stop thinking about how much he wanted that second piece of meat. So he decided on a way to get the meat from the water.

He walked back over the bridge and went down beside the water. He leaned over as far as he could, and stretched and stretched until he finally reached the place where he had seen the meat. When he opened his mouth to grasp it, the meat already in his mouth fell out and sank to the bottom of the stream. He climbed back onto the shore with a mouth full of water but no meat at all. Alas, the dog had lost everything and went home hungry.

Be thou content with what thou hast in thy hand
and thy possession; envy not that which is another's.

— SOLOMON, PROVERBS 13.7

Source ~ "The Dog's Reflection" is an animal fable from twelfth-century France.

———

"To be rich is to be happy with what one has." Pirkei Avot, "Ethics of the Fathers," a tractate of the Mishnah.

———

Yod, the tenth letter of the alphabet, has a value of ten and symbolizes creation and the spiritual world to come, even though it is barely larger than a dot.

The Lion and The Mouse

*S*ource ~ "The Lion and the Mouse" is an animal fable from twelfth-century France.

Once upon a time a great lion lay sleeping in his lair. It so happened that a tiny mouse scurried into the lion's den by accident. In his hurry to escape, he stumbled over the lion's foot and awakened him. The lion turned to see who had dared to step upon the foot of so great a king as himself. When the lion saw the tiny mouse standing beside him he thought, "That stupid

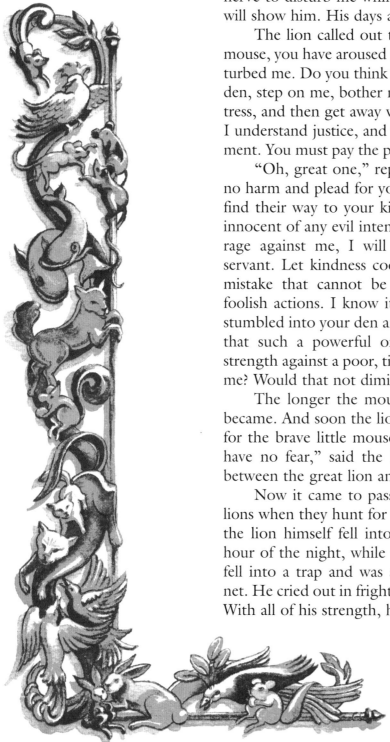

little mouse. How can such a lowly creature have the nerve to disturb me while I sleep? I, the king of beasts, will show him. His days are over."

The lion called out to the mouse, "Hey, you, little mouse, you have aroused me from my sleep and have disturbed me. Do you think that you can just come into my den, step on me, bother me like this, cause me such distress, and then get away with it? I think not, stupid one! I understand justice, and your behavior requires punishment. You must pay the penalty. Your sentence is death."

"Oh, great one," replied the mouse, "I meant you no harm and plead for your forgiveness. May my words find their way to your kind and loving heart, for I am innocent of any evil intent. If you do not let your anger rage against me, I will remain forever your humble servant. Let kindness cool your anger lest you make a mistake that cannot be undone. I am sorry for my foolish actions. I know it was wrong to have carelessly stumbled into your den and awakened you. Is it possible that such a powerful one as yourself would use his strength against a poor, tiny, defenseless little mouse like me? Would that not diminish your own greatness?"

The longer the mouse spoke, the calmer the lion became. And soon the lion began to feel some affection for the brave little mouse. "Rest easy, little friend, and have no fear," said the lion. And so there was peace between the great lion and the little mouse.

Now it came to pass, in the season of the roaring lions when they hunt for their prey in the darkness, that the lion himself fell into grave danger. In the darkest hour of the night, while the lion roamed the forest, he fell into a trap and was soon helplessly entangled in a net. He cried out in fright, but no one came to help him. With all of his strength, he tried again and again to free

himself from the snare, but the harder he pulled, the more the ropes tightened around him. He struggled and struggled until his strength was gone. Just when he was about to lose heart, he made one last anguished cry for help.

From afar the mouse was awakened by this desperate cry for help and went to the pit from which it came. The mouse yelled down, "Who is it that has awakened me from my sleep?"

"It is I, lion," came the answer. "I am ensnared in this trap of ropes. Please help me."

The mouse peered into the pit and saw that it was indeed the lion, and that he seemed to be hopelessly trapped.

"Now is the time for me to return the kindness you showed to me in your den," the mouse said to the lion. "It is in my power to help you out of this trap, and I shall return shortly with my fellow mice."

"Do hurry, mouse!" the lion pleaded, "Wisdom is better than strength. You will be more righteous than I if those you bring free me from this trap."

The mouse did as he had promised. He assembled the mice and asked them to use their teeth to chew through the ropes and cut the nets. When the lion was freed he said to the mouse, "You have saved me and I shall be grateful to you always. I look forward to the time when I can reward you with another good deed."

The mouse made a little bow and said, "Now you are free and may continue on your way." The mouse returned home to his sleep and the lion went home to his lair, both feeling safer due to the new friends they had made.

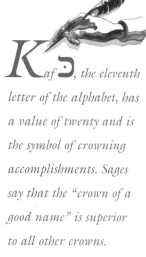

Kaf כ, *the eleventh letter of the alphabet, has a value of twenty and is the symbol of crowning accomplishments. Sages say that the "crown of a good name" is superior to all other crowns.*

"There is a time and occasion when every creature will prevail."

— FOX FABLES

The Fox and the Crow

Once there was a hungry fox searching in the forest for something delicious to eat. High up in a tree, perched on one of the branches, he spied a nice fat crow. The crow looked like such a tempting morsel that the fox decided to use his most persuasive words to coax him down to within reach. But the crow was old and much too wise to fall for the tricks of the fox. He did not budge from his branch, but just looked down at the fox with scorn.

"Crow," said the fox in a sweet manner, "it is foolish to be afraid of me. You have no reason to fear. Have you not heard that the Messiah is coming and that the birds and the beasts no longer have to be enemies?"

The crow continued to watch the fox with suspicion.

"Now if you were a Talmud scholar," continued the

fox, "as I am, you would know that the Prophet Isaiah has said that when the Messiah comes, 'the lion shall lie down with the lamb, and the fox with the crow, and there shall be peace forevermore.'"

As the fox was speaking, a pack of howling dogs approached. When the fox became aware of them he began to tremble. Fearing for his life, the fox turned and ran into the forest.

"Dear fox," yelled the crow after him, "why do you tremble in fear? And why do you run? If you believe what you say, as a learned Talmud scholar, surely you have no reason to be afraid of the animals. You know what the Prophet Isaiah has said."

As the fox dashed into the woods he called back to the crow, "Oh, it is true what the Prophet Isaiah has said, but you see, I do not think that the dogs know it yet." And with that the fox was gone.

Source ~ "The Fox and the Crow" is an animal fable from seventeenth-century Germany.

Lamed ל, the twelfth letter of the alphabet, has a value of thirty, and symbolizes heartfelt teaching, learning and education. Lamed is at the center of the alphabet and stands the tallest.

The Moon in the Well

Once upon a time a fox said to a wolf, "I have an excellent suggestion for you if you want to enjoy a really delicious meal. But you must follow my instructions very carefully."

"If there is a good meal to be had," said the wolf licking his lips, "I will do exactly as you say."

"You must go to the home of a Jew on a Friday, and offer to help him in his preparations for the Sabbath. I can assure you that if you offer your help to him, he will reward you by asking you to be a guest at the Sabbath feast."

"Hmmm," said the wolf, "this does sound like an easy way to get a good meal. I am happy that you have shared this wise advice with me, fox. You can be sure that I will follow your instructions."

And so the wolf searched until he found a Jewish home. As soon as he entered the courtyard, all the members of the household rushed out of the house, and

Source ~ "The Moon in the Well" is an animal fable from seventeenth-century Germany.

101

ran toward him waving sticks and brooms. They gave him such a severe beating that the wolf barely managed to escape with his life.

Now, the wolf was absolutely furious and went to see the fox. He was so angry about being talked into such a dangerous scheme, that he was quite prepared to tear the fox from limb to limb. But the fox calmed him and told him of another plan that was sure to work.

"You should not get so upset, wolf," said the fox, "It is not I who is to blame for the beating you got; it is really your own father who is at fault! Now listen, pay close attention to what I'm about to tell you."

The wolf then told the fox this story: "One day a Jew went to your father and asked for his help in the preparations for the Sabbath. Your father helped him, but when it came time for the meal, your father refused to wait for the blessing. Before anyone else had a chance to eat, he devoured every morsel on every plate of every course that had been so carefully prepared. He didn't even leave one little chicken bone."

The wolf quieted down, and the fox continued, "I think that you can understand now why the Jew and his family beat you when they saw you come to help with the Sabbath. Don't lose heart. I have another plan that is sure to work. I'll lead you to another house where we can both have our fill of a delicious feast."

Thoughts of the delicious feast the fox was promising filled the wolf's head, so he agreed to go along with the fox's new plan.

The fox led the wolf to a garden in which there was a well. Over the well hung two buckets suspended from ropes. When one bucket went down the other one came up. The fox climbed into one bucket and quickly fell to the bottom of the well.

The curious wolf peered down into the well. "What are you doing there?" he yelled to the fox.

"It is wonderful! You can't imagine all the good things there are to eat down here. I've never seen anything like this before. Meats, cheeses, breads, everything you can imagine. Look down into the well and you'll see for yourself."

The wolf looked into the well. Sure enough, way down at the bottom he saw a beautiful, big, round cheese! His mouth was watering and he wanted that cheese more than he wanted anything in the world. What the wolf really saw was the reflection of the moon in the water, but he believed that it was cheese.

The wolf could no longer control himself. "How can I get down there with you?" he called to the fox.

"This is the easy part, wolf. All you need to do is climb into the bucket at the top of the well, and you'll join me in a flash."

So the wolf quickly climbed into the bucket and immediately fell down to the bottom of the well. At the same time, the bucket holding the fox came back up to the top of the well. The fox jumped nimbly out of the bucket and onto the ground.

Terror seized the wolf when he realized what had happened.

"Help!" he yelled up to the fox, "How can I get out of here?"

The fox answered him by reading from the Book of Proverbs:

The righteous will be shown the way out of trouble, while the wicked will be shown the way in.

*M*em מ, *the thirteenth letter of the alphabet, has a value of forty, and is the symbol of revealed and concealed knowledge. Moses spent forty days and nights on Mount Sinai to receive the Written and Oral Laws of the Torah.*

The Rabbi and the Lion

Source ~ "The Rabbi and the Lion" is a folk legend from ancient Jerusalem.

The crest of modern Jerusalem shows the side view of a lion standing on its hind legs in front of an ancient stone wall.

Long ago in the city of Jerusalem lived a wise and righteous rabbi. One day, the people of his community decided to send him on a journey to Egypt to collect funds for the poor and needy. So the rabbi set out for the city of Hebron where he hoped to join a camel caravan. He soon found a caravan that was about to travel through the Negev desert and on to Egypt. Knowing that this journey often took up to two weeks, the rabbi arranged with the leader of the caravan to rest on Shabbat. To insure that these arrangements would be honored, the rabbi gave the caravan leader a large sum of money. Then the rabbi joined the rest of the travelers, and they all set off on their journey to Egypt.

Day after day they traveled slowly across the dry and dusty desert. On the afternoon before Shabbat, the rabbi asked the leader to stop the caravan as had been arranged. The leader ignored the rabbi and waved his

request away. The rabbi asked him again and again. The leader then sharply told him that it was wrong to stop the whole caravan for just one man. As the day drew on and the shadows grew longer, the rabbi realized that he faced a terrible dilemma: Should he continue his journey on Shabbat, or remain behind, alone in the wilderness and at the mercy of the desert beasts?

"If I stay behind, there is only a slim chance that I shall remain alive," thought the rabbi. "But if I dishonor the Shabbat by continuing on the journey, then, without any doubt, I will lose my place in the world to come." After thinking the problem through, the rabbi stopped his camel, dismounted, and with his bag in his hand, waved the caravan on.

The other travelers looked at him questioningly. Some even poked fun at him and called him a foolish old man. Others, worried about his safety, tried to get him to change his mind. They said they feared the terrible fate that awaited a man alone in the desert. But the rabbi did not change his mind, and soon the caravan continued on its way. The travelers waved goodbye, feeling certain they would never again see the famous rabbi.

When night fell, the rabbi turned his face toward Jerusalem and prayed. He then took out of his bag a small bottle of wine and a *challah*. He made the *kiddush*, ate the bread, and sang the Shabbat songs, as though he was home at his family table. Suddenly, he saw a huge lion standing directly in front of him. A cold shiver of terror ran down his spine. But as he looked more closely at the lion, he noticed that the beast was looking at him with friendly eyes. So the rabbi continued his meal and resumed singing the Shabbat songs with his usual joy and enthusiasm.

The lion stood quietly by, seeming to listen to the rabbi, then stretched out on the sand and went to sleep. Millions of stars looked down on the desert that night. The rabbi said his prayers, then lay down and, in the quiet and peace of the desert night, was soon fast asleep. When he woke up the next morning the lion was standing nearby watching him with interest. Then the rabbi understood! The lion had been sent by God to protect him from the dangers of the desert night. The rabbi spent the rest of Shabbat in prayer, and celebrated the final Shabbat meal with the last of his bread. He was fully confident that the Lord would help him find his way to safety.

When Shabbat came to an end, the rabbi said the evening prayer and made *havdalah* over the wine. At that very moment the lion got up, shook his mane, gently licked the rabbi's hand, and stretched out on the ground beside him. The rabbi understood that the lion was inviting him to climb onto his back. Without a moment's hesitation, the rabbi mounted the lion's back, which was as soft as a pillow, held on tightly to the lion's mane, and off they rode toward Egypt. Thus, the lion and the rabbi, with his black robes billowing in the wind, flew through the desert night.

By dawn the next morning they had caught up with the caravan. The travelers were amazed. They watched speechlessly as the lion and his rider approached. The lion gently knelt down to let the rabbi off, then rose, let out a terrifying roar, and tore off into the desert. The leader of the caravan fell to his knees, saying how sorry he was to have offended the holy man. He pleaded with the rabbi to forgive his wrongdoing, and this the rabbi did.

To this day the rabbi is called Rabbi Ariel, because a lion, *(Ari)* of God *(el)*, protected and saved him.

*C*hallah is a special white bread, usually braided, for Sabbath and holiday meals.

Kiddush is a ceremonial blessing that is said over bread or wine.

Havdalah is the ceremony marking the close of the Sabbath or other holy days.

"Remember the sabbath day, to keep it holy."
— EXODUS 20.8

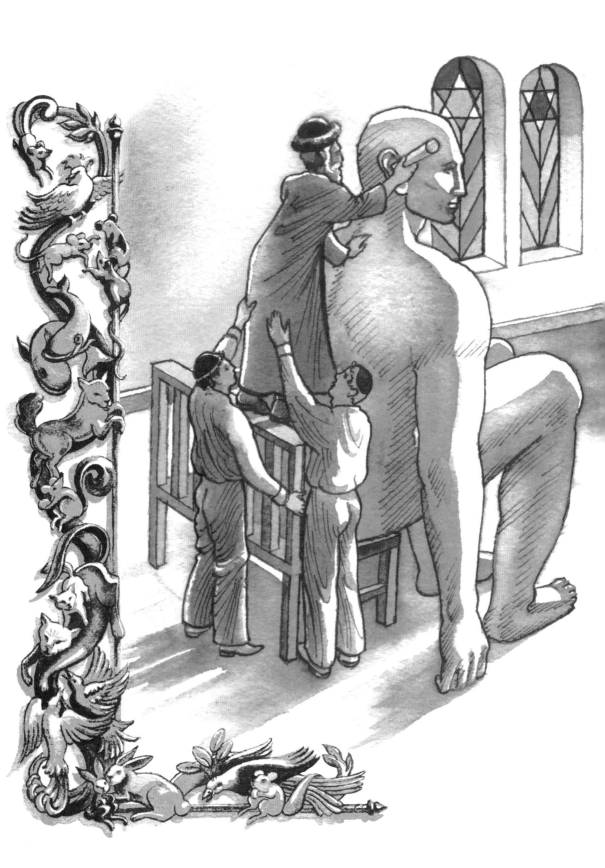

The Golem of Vilna

Legend tells us that long ago the wisest rabbis knew the secret Name of God. With this knowledge they could create words, move mountains, and even make living creatures out of clay. These living creatures were called golems, and this is the tale of the Golem of Vilna.

Long ago the Vilna Gaon, one of the greatest and wisest rabbis of Eastern Europe, may his name be

*S*ource ~ "The Golem of Vilna" is a folk legend from seventeenth-century Eastern Europe.

The golem legends are among the most famous of the folklore of the Middle Ages and may have been one of the inspirations for Mary Shelley's Frankenstein.

blessed in heaven, saw a need to take extraordinary measures to protect the Jews of his community. The Jews of Vilna were in constant danger from unruly mobs, both in the public markets and in their homes. Thus, they were often injured and often lacked food and other necessities. The Vilna Gaon thought the time had come to create a golem.

The Gaon was a learned scholar, who knew by heart the five Books of Moses, the Commentaries, and all the secrets of the kabbalah. He also knew the secret Name of Names, the Name of God. With all his knowledge he started to form a golem from sand and clay. By adding water, a little at a time, his creation began to look like a man, a very large man. After the Vilna Gaon had finished shaping his creation, he wrote the secret Name of God on a piece of paper and tucked the paper into the golem's ear. Thus, the golem was transformed into a living being.

Because the power of speech is God's alone to give, the golem could not speak, but he could understand all the instructions given him. He had excellent eyesight, and his sense of hearing was so good that he was able to detect sounds from a great distance. He was also a creature of many disguises, and could drift through the air like a breeze on a cold day. Indeed, there was very little he could not do. There was just one problem. The golem sometimes got carried away when he performed his tasks and so he had to be carefully watched, like the day the rabbi had asked the golem to bring water from the well to the kitchen. The golem brought bucket after bucket after bucket, until the kitchen was flooded with water. Only the rabbi's command to stop sent the golem back to his own corner of the house.

The golem's most important function was to help faithful Jews on holidays and market days. When there was a great shortage of food in the marketplace and the Jews could not provide for their Shabbas meals, the Vilna Gaon sent the golem into the river. Because the golem was safe from drowning and knew the language of fish, the Gaon instructed him to venture far out into the water, call the fish together, tie them up in a net and bring them back to shore. He then told the golem to distribute the fish to the families. The golem did this by leaping from house to house like a bird.

One day, as the Jews were shopping in the main square, they were attacked by an angry mob of peasants. They threw stones at the Jews, beat them with sticks, and set their homes on fire. The Gaon sent for the golem and turned him loose. Ah, how the golem went to work! He cracked the attackers' heads and broke their arms and legs. The peasants could not hurt the golem because they could not catch him, nor could they escape from him. When the mayor of Vilna heard about these happenings, he begged the rabbi to stop the golem so that peace could be restored. The Gaon agreed to do so upon the mayor's promise to protect the Jews from that day forward. The mayor agreed and kept his promise.

When the Gaon saw that the marketplace was once again well stocked, that even the poorest family in his community had enough food for the Shabbas feast, and that peace had been restored, he decided that the golem was no longer needed. He removed from the golem's ear the bit of paper with the Name of Names on it, and the golem vanished. The Jews of Vilna hoped they would never again need a golem, but trusted that there would always be a rabbi who could create one should the need arise.

Legend says that Rabbi Löw of Prague, the mystical and beloved sixteenth-century gaon, created a golem. Visitors today tuck special notes and messages for the Rabbi into the ancient stones around his gravesite in Prague, just as they've done for centuries.

The Story of Abraham

Long, long ago, ten generations after the flood, the Lord, blessed be He, looked down upon the earth and chose to speak to the shepherd Abram in a dream. The day after the dream, Abram stood in front of his tent and wondered about the strange message he had received from God. Tall, sunburned and strong, he gazed out over his many herds of sheep, and the shepherds tending them.

His wife, Sarai, came out of the tent and stood beside him. "What are you thinking about, Abram?"

"I am thinking of the dream I had last night," he replied. "I was standing alone in a field when suddenly I heard the voice of God. 'Abram, leave your country and go from your father's house to the west. There you will find a land of green pastures and silver streams. I will bless you, and you will become the father of a great nation.'"

"Is there such a land?" asked Sarai.

"Yes," said Abram, "Look! What do you see, far in the distance?"

"Mountaintops," she answered.

"Beyond those mountains is the land of which God spoke. Tomorrow we shall rise with the dawn and begin our journey."

Abram blew a shrill whistle to call the leader of the shepherds, his nephew Lot.

"Herd all the sheep and cattle together," he instructed Lot, "and ask the servants to pack up the tents and all our household goods. We leave this place at dawn."

"Where are we going, Abram?" asked Lot.

"To the mountains, to a new country; a country where I can worship the one Almighty God in peace."

At dawn, Abram mounted his camel to begin the journey to his new home. He rode at the head of the caravan with Sarai at his side. The shepherds with their wives and children followed behind. The caravan moved slowly so that the sheep and goats could be kept together. They traveled for many days until they came to the great mountains.

"Let us stop here," Abram said.

The animals were unloaded, the tents set up, and fires were built, while Abram climbed to the top of the mountain alone. There, he built an altar to God and prayed.

Abram then summoned Lot to the top of the mountain. They looked at the vast country spread before them. Their cattle and sheep covered the mountain like a blanket. Then Abram and Lot heard the shepherds quarreling over the grasslands.

"Get your cattle out of the way!" shouted Lot's shepherds angrily. "Leave some grass for us!"

"The grass grows all around for miles. Find another pasture land for your herds!" yelled Abram's shepherds. "Take your cattle away, or we will drive them off!"

When Abram heard the shepherds' angry threats, he ran down from the mountaintop crying, "Peace! Peace! This is no time for quarrels."

At the sound of Abram's gentle but commanding voice, the shepherds stopped quarreling.

"Look at the beautiful country all around us," said Abram. "We are brothers. There is too much land here for us to be quarreling over pastures. Let us each go a

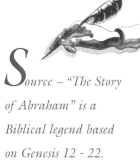

*S*ource ~ "The Story of Abraham" is a Biblical legend based on Genesis 12 - 22.

_____

Abraham, the founder of the Israelite religion in the land of Canaan, is said to have lived between 2000-1500 B.C.E.

113

different way. Lot, look around you. Which do you choose? Right or left?"

Lot looked out over the plain to the beautiful river Jordan flowing through the center of the land. He saw two beautiful cities, Sodom and Gomorrah. "There! I choose the plain of the river Jordan," he said.

So Lot gathered all that belonged to him and traveled east.

After Lot had gone Abram heard the voice of God. "Abram, look to the east, look to the west, look to the north, and look to the south. All the land that you see I give to you and your children forever. Rise and walk the distance of this land for it belongs to you."

As God had told him to do, Abram walked the length and width of the land. He finally came to rest under some large oak trees, in a place called Hebron. Here he made his home and built an altar to the Lord.

Abram was awakened one night by the barking of his camp's watchdogs. When he stepped out of his tent, a man fell to his knees before him. His clothes were torn and his body was bruised.

"Who are you?" asked Abram.

"I've come from Sodom," replied the man breathlessly. "Lot has been captured. The cities of Sodom and Gomorrah are being attacked and the inhabitants are being carried off as slaves. I alone escaped. The kingdoms around you have been captured. The enemy is now close to you."

When Abram heard this terrible news he called for all the men in the camp to gather at once and prepare to march against the enemy. Within a few hours, Abram led three hundred well-armed men to ambush the invaders right in the midst of their victory celebrations. They drove them far into the wilderness, freed their prisoners,

and returned all the stolen goods to their rightful owners in Sodom. Then Abram found Lot and his family.

The king of Sodom was so grateful to Abram for saving his people that he wanted to reward him. But Abram said, "I want no reward. I came to rescue my nephew Lot and his family. Now that they are safe, I ask for nothing more. You have all suffered enough at the hands of your enemy." The people honored Abram and thanked him for his kindness. The king, a priest of God, brought Abram bread and wine, then said "Blessed be Abram of the God most high, Maker of heaven and earth."

Soon thereafter, the Lord appeared to Abram again and told him he was to enter into an everlasting covenant with him. The Lord said, "Abram, you are to be the father of many nations. Kings will be born of you. From this day forth, you are to be known as Abraham, a father of many nations."

"I bless your wife, who shall be known as Sarah, a mother of nations," said the Lord. "She shall bear a son, whom you will call Isaac." Abraham and Sarah were very old and had long given up the hope of having children together. Sarah, knowing of Abraham's great longing for a son, had arranged for her maidservant, Hagar, to be Abraham's second wife, and they had a son, Ishmael. But the miracle came to pass, just as the Lord had said, and Sarah gave birth to a boy, whom they called Isaac. He grew into a strong and healthy boy, deeply loved by Abraham and Sarah.

One night Abraham heard the voice of God calling him, "Abraham, you must take Isaac into the land of Moriah. At the top of a high mountain you must sacrifice Isaac to me." Abraham was stunned. He could not sleep the rest of that night. He tossed and turned and

The Midrash tells us that God took the letter Hei from under his Throne of Glory and placed it in the middle of Abram's name, renaming him Abraham, as a reward for recognizing God as the One Creator of heaven and earth.

The traditional meaning of Isaac is "one who laughs."

waited for dawn. He was overwhelmed with sadness because he knew that he must follow God's command.

With the first signs of morning, he awakened two servant boys and told them to load the donkeys with food and firewood. He awakened Isaac and told him to prepare for a long journey. He said nothing to Sarah.

"Where are we going, Father?" asked Isaac.

"To the land of Moriah," answered Abraham sadly, hiding his face so that the boy would not see his tears. He was so disturbed by God's commandment, and not at all sure what he would do, that he could say no more to his son. He led the way silently.

They traveled for three days. At last they came to Mount Moriah. High above the other peaks, its top seemed lost in the clouds.

"This is the mountain," said Abraham. "Both of you boys stay here with the donkeys while Isaac and I climb up the mountain to make a sacrifice."

Isaac took wood and followed behind his father as he climbed up the steep mountain path.

"Father, we have wood and fire, but how can we make a sacrifice without a lamb?"

"God will give us a lamb for a sacrifice," answered Abraham. They climbed higher and higher until they reached a flat space of ground.

"We will make our sacrifice here," said Abraham. He built an altar, piling it high with wood. Then, his hand trembling and his eyes blinded by tears, he took his son Isaac and laid him on the altar. Suddenly the voice of God called from Heaven, "Abraham, Abraham!"

"I am here Lord," answered Abraham.

"Do not lay your hand on your son! I do not want a child sacrificed. Now I know how much you love God. You would not even keep your son from me."

Abraham fell to the ground and wept. Isaac was dearer to him than anything in the world. Just then he heard a noise and looked around to see a young ram caught by its horns in the bushes.

Abraham caught the ram and placed it on the altar as a sacrifice. He kissed his son and said, "I shall call this place 'In the mount where the Lord is seen.'"

God said, "Because you were willing to give me your beloved son, I bless you and all who come after you, for you have listened to my voice. I promise your children will number as many as the stars in Heaven and the sands on the seashore, and they will become a great nation."

Abraham was so happy that he kissed Isaac again and again. They climbed down the mountain and returned home.

And so it came to pass that human life was held sacred from this time on. Abraham remained faithful to his mission of a better way of life for his people, and dedicated his life to God.

Christians, Muslims, and Jews acknowledge Abraham as the person- ification of a man of unswerving faith.

The Tower of Babel

Long, long ago, after the great flood, when all the people of the earth spoke one language, the descendants of Noah had been ravaged by many battles. To save their community, the people's council wanted to build a new city around a tall tower that would reach so high into the sky, it would touch the heavens. "We wish to become known throughout the world for our great tower," they said when they presented their ideas to King Nimrod. "From the heights of the tower we will be able to see our enemies before they see us, destroy them with great force, and rule the earth." Nimrod was impressed and approved the plan.

And so representatives of the council journeyed to seek out the perfect place for their new city. After two years they came upon the land of Shinar, where they found that perfect place — a beautiful valley with a spacious flat plane.

The council gathered together the families of the community, and together they migrated to the land of Shinar to begin their new life.

Source ~ "The Tower of Babel" is an aggadah from a Midrash based on Genesis 11:1-9

The Hebrew word "bilbul" means confusion.

The word Babel also means "gate of God," and gives us the word babble.

Soon bricks were baked in giant ovens until they were harder than rocks, dirt was mixed with water to make mortar, and the building began.

The tower grew so high that those carrying bricks and mortar up the giant ramps had to climb for a full year before they reached the top. Workers climbed day and night, day after day and night after night. The entire span of the growing tower was always filled with workers – some climbing up and some coming down.

The people's pride grew with each brick laid, as did their anticipation of the power they would possess once the tower was completed. Little by little, pride gave way to arrogance, and soon the people viewed themselves as greater and stronger than their Lord God in heaven. There were those who wanted to wage war with all who dwelt in heaven; those who wanted to place their own gods in heaven and do service only unto them; and others who wanted to smite the Lord Himself. The builders became obsessed with the growing tower. Nothing else mattered. When a co-worker accidentally fell off the tower, there was less concern for his life than for any bricks that may have fallen with him.

And it came to pass that Abraham heard of the mighty tower being built, and so he traveled to the valley of Shinar. He saw how the tower had changed the people, how it had poisoned their hearts and minds. He tried to stop the building, but no one listened. Abraham prayed to the Lord: "God Almighty, stop the building of this tower and scatter these people through-out the world." The Lord summoned some of his trusted angels and sent them down to the new city to create confusion, and so they did.

Suddenly every builder spoke a different language, and no one on the tower could understand anyone else.

When a man asked for a brick, his co-worker handed him mortar; when a builder asked for mortar, he got a hammer instead. Frustration grew and soon workers were flinging bricks and mortar at one another, builders were falling from the tower, one after the other, and a great many died.

Thus, the Lord punished all those who had rebelled against Him. The ones who had threatened heaven with arrows perished at the hands of their co-workers; those who had wanted to place their own gods in heaven were turned into wild animals; and those who had wanted to smite the Lord Himself were dispersed throughout the world. The rest of the people in the community were spared. They stopped work on the tower and left the land of Shinar forever.

Fire fell from heaven and burned the top of the tower, and a great earthquake swallowed the bottom. The part of the tower that remained stands to this day, exposed to the winds of heaven, and casts a shadow that is many, many miles long.

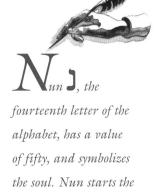

Nun ‏נ‎, the fourteenth letter of the alphabet, has a value of fifty, and symbolizes the soul. Nun starts the Hebrew word for candle, "ner," often a symbol for the soul, or the divine spark within the individual.

The Mysterious Palace

King Solomon had many treasures. One of his favorites was a magic carpet many miles long and woven of golden thread. A secret command from the King would lift the carpet into the air and send it sailing through the sky to distant exotic lands.

One day the King gathered his attendants, got on the carpet, and took off on a journey. As the carpet soared high above the earth, the King swelled with pride, and thought, "The Holy and Blessed One has made me ruler of all His creatures. There is no one in the world as wise as I am."

Suddenly a powerful wind came and tipped the carpet to one side. The King and his companions were so violently jarred that they almost fell off the carpet. King Solomon became angry and commanded the wind to stop. "Indeed, great King, I will do as you wish," answered the wind, "but you must always remember my power, and stop your prideful ways. You are only a man made of flesh and blood who will one day turn to dust. Now, hold on tightly to your carpet for I am going to carry you far away." Then a strong gust of air blew across the carpet. The carpet billowed like a sail and moved swiftly ahead. It soared through the vast heavens for many nights and many days, and finally came to rest on a mountain beside a palace of gleaming gold. The King and his court stepped from the carpet and stared in wonder at the incredible site before them.

King Solomon said, "I have never seen anything to compare with this palace. Come, let us enter and see what is within."

The King and his company approached the palace, but discovered that high walls surrounded it. They could find no door or gateway of any kind. The King commanded one of his attendants to climb onto the roof to see if there was an entry. The attendant found only a large eagle tending its chicks. He climbed back down and told the King about the great bird. King Solomon, who could speak the language of birds, called to the eagle in its own language. The eagle swiftly swooped down to stand before him, and sang a hymn of praise to Solomon, calling him the Holy and Blessed One, the King of all Kings, and then graciously bowed.

"What is your name?" asked the King.

"My name is Elanod."

"Elanod, do you know whether or not this palace has an entrance?"

"No, my lord, I do not. I have never heard of one, nor have I seen one." replied the eagle.

"And how old are you, Elanod?"

"My lord King, I am seven hundred years old."

"How can we find out about the entrance to this palace?" asked King Solomon.

"I have a brother who is two hundred years older than I. Perhaps he can help you."

Thereupon the King ordered the eagle to summon his brother. Before long, another great eagle arrived. It, too, bowed down before Solomon, and sang the hymn praising the Holy and Blessed One who is King of all Kings.

"What is your name, eagle?" Solomon asked him.

"Alof is my name."

"Alof, do you know about the entrance to this golden palace?"

"No, my lord King. That I do not know, but I have

Source ~ "The Mysterious Palace" is a fifth-century fairy tale from the Babylonian region of the ancient country of Mesopotamia.

a brother who is four hundred years older than I am. Perhaps he can help you."

At the King's command, Alof soared away to summon his brother, and after a long, long time a third great eagle stood before Solomon. This eagle was very, very old and could barely move his giant wings. He greeted the King with the same hymn in praise of the Holy and Blessed One, the King of Kings, and then bowed low to Solomon.

"Eagle, by what name are you known?" asked the King.

"Altaamor."

"Altaamor, can you tell me of an entrance to this golden palace?"

"No, my lord King, I have never seen an entrance. My father told me there was once an entrance in the western wall that over the centuries of time has been covered up by dust and earth. If you command the wind to remove the earth, the entrance will appear."

Solomon summoned the wind and asked it to remove the dust and earth from the western wall. The wind huffed and puffed and blew with all its force. Once, twice, three times, and the entrance appeared! A large iron gate protected the opening. Over the top of the gate these words appeared: "O sons of men, be it known to you that within this palace we dwelt. There was delight and pleasure for all within. Then a great famine befell us and we ate ground pearls instead of wheat. We were not sustained and were doomed to perish."

Solomon then found another message that was written on the lock of the gate: "No man may enter this palace unless he is a prophet or a king." To the right of the gate stood a glass box containing the keys to the palace. Solomon took the keys, opened the gate, and

entered the palace. The walls of the palace were covered with brilliant rubies, emeralds, and sapphires that had been set in gold.

King Solomon went from room to room, each brighter and more exquisite than the one before. When he came to the seventh room, he saw an enormous crystal statue. On either side of it was a marble pillar, and beneath the statue were engraved these words: "I am Shaddad, son of Aad, and I reigned over countless thousands of warriors; yet, when the Angel of Death came for me, I could not prevail against him. Therefore, son of man, know that you shall not take lightly the cares of the world, for in the end every man will turn to dust and return to his true home. The most important thing he leaves behind is his good name."

Solomon now understood what the wind had meant, and he knew that the wind was right. He returned to his palace in Jerusalem and, from that day forward, devoted himself to a life of good deeds.

This legend is considered to be the story of Solomon's inspiration to write down his thoughts. He is traditionally credited as the writer of Ecclesiastes, Proverbs and Song of Solomon.

"To everything there is a season, and a time to every purpose under the heaven." This is one of Solomon's sayings that remain popular today.

— ECCLESIASTES 3:1

King David and the Giant

Long, long ago the land of Israel was ruled by the mighty King David. He was as brave as he was smart, and his heart was filled with the love of God. He governed his people with justice and fairness, and his fame spread far and wide.

One day, when King David was in the forest hunting, Satan, the Prince of Darkness, appeared before him disguised as a deer. David aimed his bow, shot an arrow, but missed the deer. He shot more arrows, but none hit their target. He chased the deer and continued shooting, arrow after arrow, until he was in the land of his enemies, the Philistines. And it was in this way that Satan tricked King David and led him to the cave of the giant Ishbi-benob, the brother of Goliath.

When David was a young shepherd he had agreed to face the mighty giant Goliath in combat when no other man was brave enough to come forth. David had slain Goliath with a perfectly aimed stone from his slingshot. From that day forth, Ishbi-benob sought revenge for his brother's death.

When David passed by Ishbi-benob's cave, the giant, who had been lying in wait, jumped out and caught David off guard. The giant tied him with ropes, dragged him into his cave, and shoved him beneath an olive press. Miraculously, the ground beneath David was very soft, so he was not crushed; but he was trapped.

The King's capture had taken place on a Friday just as Abishai ben Zeruiah, David's trusted army general,

Source ~ "King David and the Giant" is a fairy tale from fifth-century Babylonia.

———

This story, based on 2 Samuel 21:16-17, is one of the twelve fairy tales found in the Talmud.

127

was preparing for the Sabbath. As Abishai was washing his hands in a basin, he noticed bloodstains in the water, and then he heard a bird's cry. He looked through his window and saw a dove perched on a branch, beating its wings back and forth. Abishai knew this was a sign and that he must try to understand its meaning. Because the dove is a symbol for Israel, Abishai was convinced that King David himself must be in danger.

Abishai left his house immediately to look for the King. He went first to the palace, then to the House of Study, and finally to the House of Prayer, but the King was nowhere to be found.

Abishai then remembered that King David possessed a magic mirror that could reveal the location of anyone or anything that was lost. He also had a magic mare, as swift as the wind. Because he had once been present when the King used his magical treasures, he knew where they were kept and how to make them work. But he also knew that the King had forbidden anyone to touch the mirror or ride the mare.

Abishai gathered the wise men of the kingdom to present his dilemma. "I have reason to believe that King David is in grave danger. The only way to find him is through his magic mirror, and the only way to reach him is with his magic mare. As you know, the king has forbidden anyone to use these possessions." After some discussion, the wise men agreed that in a time of danger such as this, it was permissible to use the King's magic.

Abishai took the magic mirror and asked to see King David. He looked into the mirror and saw that David was imprisoned under an olive press in Ishbi-benob's cave. The hideous giant was laughing triumphantly at what he thought was the King's death.

Abishai immediately jumped onto the magic mare

and rode off into the forest to find the cave. The mare galloped so swiftly that her hooves never even touched the ground. In the twinkling of an eye, Abishai stood before the opening to the great giant's cave.

Orpah, the giant's mother, was sitting outside the cave spinning thread and saw Abishai arrive. She knew that he was there to rescue King David. She stopped spinning and threw her spindle at Abishai, but the spindle missed him. Abishai picked up the spindle, threw it back at Orpah and struck her head. She fell over, dead.

Ishbi-benob came out of the cave when he heard the commotion, and roared with fury. He lifted up the olive press and threw it at Abishai. He then saw, to his amazement, that King David was still alive; he had not been crushed at all! The giant tossed the olive press aside and anchored the bottom of his tall spear into the ground. He grabbed David and flung him into the air, intending him to fall onto the spear and die. At that moment, Abishai pronounced the Holy Name of God and David froze in the air. Abishai pronounced the Divine Name again and David floated slowly to the ground, landing a safe distance from the spear.

Abishai jumped onto the mare and galloped toward David with one arm outstretched. David grabbed Abishai's arm and swung himself up onto the mare. As they swiftly flew off into the night the giant tried to chase them, but in his fury he fumbled and tripped over the olive press and fell to the ground. The olive press rolled over on him and crushed him to death.

When King David was safely back in his palace, he gave thanks to Abishai for his bravery and quick thinking. He then praised the Holy One, Blessed be He, for protecting him from danger and saving him from the terrible fate Ishbi-benob had planned for him.

David reigned as King of Judah, then of Israel, from 1000-961 B.C.E. The son of a shepherd, David was a fine musician, a valiant warrior, and an outstanding leader.

In both the Old and New Testaments the Messiah is referred to as the Son of David.

The Two Brothers

Long ago, in the land of Israel, lived two poor brothers who loved each other very much. The brothers farmed a small piece of land that they had inherited from their father. The younger brother had a family – a wife and three children; the older brother was unmarried. The brothers worked hard tilling the wheat on their small plot of land and at harvest time divided the sheaves into two equal shares.

One night, after a day of harvesting, the older brother was unable to sleep. He thought of his younger brother, of how he had to struggle to provide his wife and children with the food and clothing they needed. "I'm alone," he said to himself, "I don't need as much as my brother. He has a growing family and should have a larger share of the harvest." So at midnight he got out of bed, took a few sheaves from his own pile, and secretly added them to his brother's pile. Then, freed from worry, he returned to his bed and went to sleep.

Source ~ "The Two Brothers" is an aggadah parable of a midrash from ancient Palestine.

Samech ס, the fifteenth letter of the alphabet, has a value of sixty, and is the symbol for protection and support, as seen in its enclosing shape.

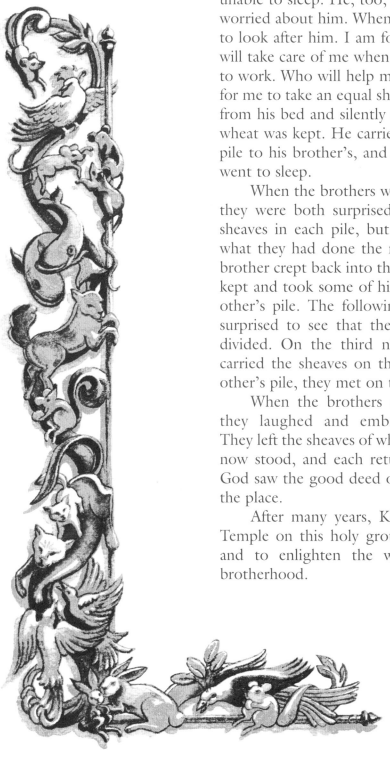

On this same night the younger brother was also unable to sleep. He, too, thought of his brother. "I am worried about him. When he is old there will be no one to look after him. I am fortunate to have children who will take care of me when I no longer have the strength to work. Who will help my brother then? It is not right for me to take an equal share of the harvest." So he rose from his bed and silently crept into the shed where the wheat was kept. He carried some sheaves from his own pile to his brother's, and then returned to his bed and went to sleep.

When the brothers went to work the next morning they were both surprised to see the same number of sheaves in each pile, but they did not tell each other what they had done the night before. That night each brother crept back into the shed where the sheaves were kept and took some of his own and added them to the other's pile. The following morning, they were again surprised to see that the piles of wheat were equally divided. On the third night, however, as they again carried the sheaves on their shoulders to bring to the other's pile, they met on the way.

When the brothers realized what had happened, they laughed and embraced with warm affection. They left the sheaves of wheat on the ground where they now stood, and each returned to his own bed. When God saw the good deed of the two brothers he blessed the place.

After many years, King Solomon built the Great Temple on this holy ground to hold the holy tablets, and to enlighten the world with peace, love, and brotherhood.

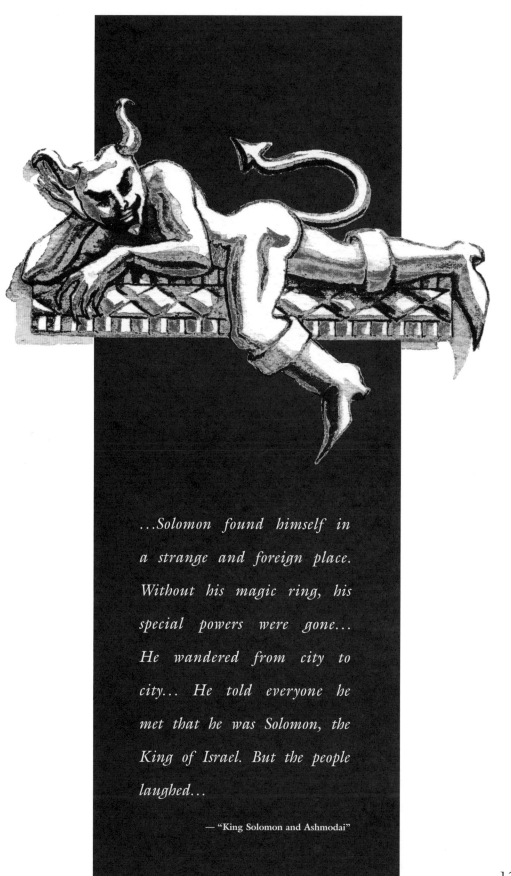

...*Solomon found himself in a strange and foreign place. Without his magic ring, his special powers were gone... He wandered from city to city... He told everyone he met that he was Solomon, the King of Israel. But the people laughed...*

— "King Solomon and Ashmodai"

Fourth to Sixth Grades

SIXTH GRADE

King Solomon and Ashmodai

Long ago, the great King Solomon, may he rest in peace, ruled the ancient land of Israel. The source of Solomon's powers was a magic ring on which the secret Name of God was engraved. When Solomon built the Temple he hired the finest craftsmen and builders. He also

pressed into service the supernatural beings over whom he had been granted command. Among these was Ashmodai, the King of Demons, who could foretell the future, become invisible, and assume many disguises. Solomon had used his magic ring to summon Ashmodai to help him build the temple. To make sure that the King of Demons would be powerless against him, Solomon had him bound in chains.

When the Temple was completed, Solomon refused to release Ashmodai. Indeed, Solomon had become vain and arrogant about his extraordinary powers, his wisdom, and his magnificent wealth. He thought there was no one in the world as great as he was. Solomon was also guilty of the three things kings are warned against. First, the Bible states that a king shall not have a lot of wives; Solomon had many. Second, the Bible says a king shall not have many horses; Solomon had many herds. And third, the Bible warns that a king shall not have an abundance of gold and silver; Solomon was the richest man in the world. When the Holy One, Blessed be He, saw what was happening to Solomon, he decided to banish him to wander from place to place as a homeless beggar.

To accomplish this, the Holy One enlisted the services of the Demon King. Ashmodai told Solomon that if he could be released from his chains, he would tell him a great secret that would allow him to follow God's will and be forgiven for his sins. Solomon, who knew that Ashmodai at times performed acts of kindness, ordered the release of the Demon King. As the chains fell to the ground, Ashmodai rose up in all his great might. When his full power was restored he struck Solomon, dragged him from his throne, and pulled the magic ring from his finger. He then picked Solomon up and hurled him into space, sending him far across the kingdom. Ashmodai

Source ~ "King Solomon and Ashmodai" is a King Solomon legend from Babylonia dating from the fifth century.

This story is one of the twelve fairy tales found in the Talmud.

King Solomon received his extraordinary wisdom, riches, honor, and powers of the invisible world from God.
— 1 KINGS 4:29-31.

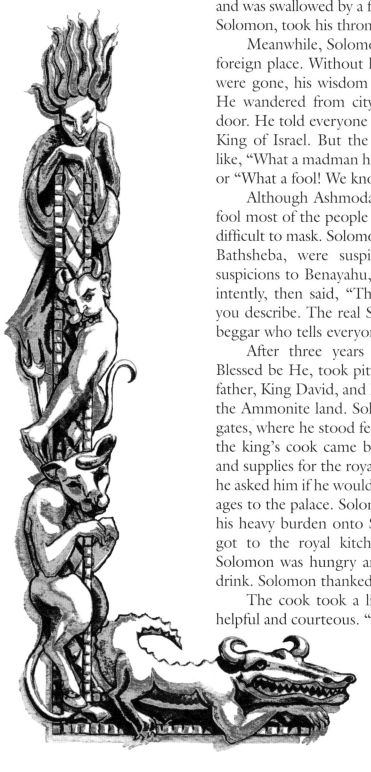

then threw the ring as far as he could. It landed in the sea and was swallowed by a fish. Ashmodai disguised himself as Solomon, took his throne, and fooled the people of Israel.

Meanwhile, Solomon found himself in a strange and foreign place. Without his magic ring, his special powers were gone, his wisdom was gone, and he was penniless. He wandered from city to city, begging from door to door. He told everyone he met that he was Solomon, the King of Israel. But the people laughed, and said things like, "What a madman he is to think he is King Solomon," or "What a fool! We know that the King is in Jerusalem."

Although Ashmodai's disguise was good enough to fool most of the people of Israel, his demonic nature was difficult to mask. Solomon's wives and Solomon's mother, Bathsheba, were suspicious. Bathsheba confided her suspicions to Benayahu, Solomon's General. He listened intently, then said, "This can only be Ashmodai whom you describe. The real Solomon must be that wandering beggar who tells everyone he meets that he is the King."

After three years of wandering, the Holy One, Blessed be He, took pity on Solomon for the sake of his father, King David, and led him to Rabbath, the capital of the Ammonite land. Solomon found himself at the city's gates, where he stood feeling sad and lonely. After a while the king's cook came by carrying large bundles of food and supplies for the royal kitchen. When he saw Solomon he asked him if he would be willing to help carry the packages to the palace. Solomon agreed, and the cook shifted his heavy burden onto Solomon's shoulders. When they got to the royal kitchen, the cook, recognizing that Solomon was hungry and thirsty, offered him food and drink. Solomon thanked the cook and took the offerings.

The cook took a liking to this beggar who was so helpful and courteous. "I need some help in the kitchen,"

he said. "If you would like to stay on and work with me, I can offer you room and board." And so Solomon remained with the Ammonites. He worked hard, practiced everything the royal cook taught him, and learned his skills well. He was soon able to create and prepare many delicious dishes.

One day Solomon asked the cook if he could have the honor of preparing the king's dinner. The cook replied, "Your craft has been well learned and your talent is obvious — go right ahead!" Solomon cooked a glorious meal for the king. When the king finished eating, he entered the royal kitchen — an unusual event — and asked, "Who cooked my dinner tonight? I have never tasted anything so delicious!"

The royal cook bowed and said, "Your Highness, my assistant did."

When the king asked to meet the assistant, Solomon stepped forward and bowed to the Ammonite ruler, who said, "It pleases me to have you with us."

"At your service," answered Solomon.

Solomon did well in his service in the royal kitchen, and he was soon noticed by princess Ne'amah, the king's beautiful daughter. She fell in love with the cook and told her mother she wished to marry him. "Ne'amah," scolded her mother, "your father's kingdom is full of lords and noblemen. Pick one of them to be your husband."

But Ne'amah was determined. "Mother, I don't want a lord or a nobleman. I want the cook because I love him." Her mother tried hard to change her daughter's mind, but no argument would sway the princess. Over and over she said, "Mother, he's the only man in the world I want to marry!"

The queen was finally forced to tell her husband that Ne'amah wished to marry the cook. The king was so

The most famous female demon in Jewish lore is Lilith. Legend says she was Adam's first wife and left him after a quarrel. During the Middle Ages her legend took on frightening aspects; she became a night demon, with long disheveled hair and massive wings, who attempted to strangle newborn infants and seduce men. Amulets served as protection against her.

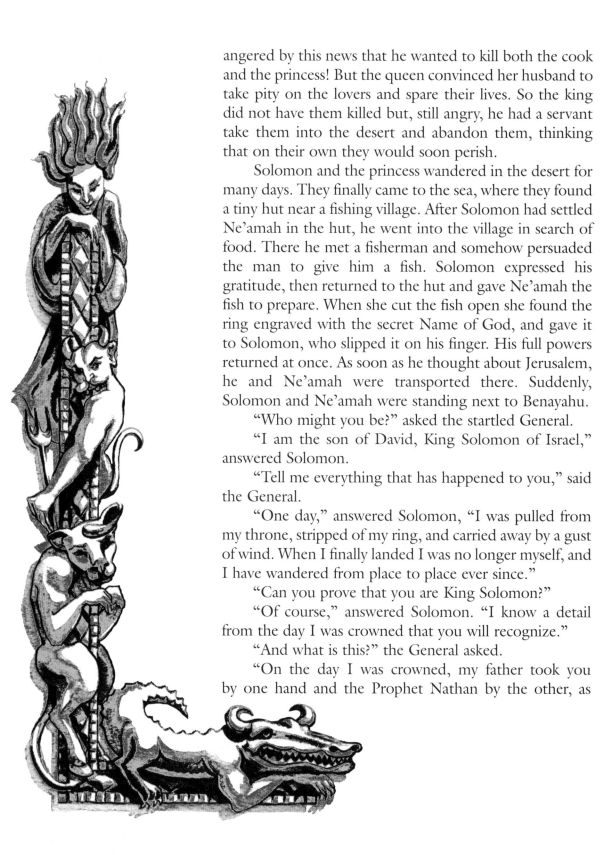

angered by this news that he wanted to kill both the cook and the princess! But the queen convinced her husband to take pity on the lovers and spare their lives. So the king did not have them killed but, still angry, he had a servant take them into the desert and abandon them, thinking that on their own they would soon perish.

Solomon and the princess wandered in the desert for many days. They finally came to the sea, where they found a tiny hut near a fishing village. After Solomon had settled Ne'amah in the hut, he went into the village in search of food. There he met a fisherman and somehow persuaded the man to give him a fish. Solomon expressed his gratitude, then returned to the hut and gave Ne'amah the fish to prepare. When she cut the fish open she found the ring engraved with the secret Name of God, and gave it to Solomon, who slipped it on his finger. His full powers returned at once. As soon as he thought about Jerusalem, he and Ne'amah were transported there. Suddenly, Solomon and Ne'amah were standing next to Benayahu.

"Who might you be?" asked the startled General.

"I am the son of David, King Solomon of Israel," answered Solomon.

"Tell me everything that has happened to you," said the General.

"One day," answered Solomon, "I was pulled from my throne, stripped of my ring, and carried away by a gust of wind. When I finally landed I was no longer myself, and I have wandered from place to place ever since."

"Can you prove that you are King Solomon?"

"Of course," answered Solomon. "I know a detail from the day I was crowned that you will recognize."

"And what is this?" the General asked.

"On the day I was crowned, my father took you by one hand and the Prophet Nathan by the other, as

mother bent down to father and kissed him."

The General called for an immediate gathering of the supreme council, the Sanhedrin. When they were assembled, General Benayahu said to its members, "Inscribe the secret Name of God over your hearts. It is Ashmodai who now sits on the throne, and we must remove him."

"But we fear the name inscribed over his heart," said the members of the council.

"Do not lose your courage," said the General. This is your chance for glory. Come, I will lead."

And Benayahu himself went to Ashmodai, caught him off guard, and struck a mighty blow to his head. At that moment a thunderous voice spoke from heaven, "Strike no more! It was my will to punish Solomon for not following the laws of the Bible. He now has atoned for his sins, and may once again sit upon his throne."

As soon as Solomon had returned to the palace and the royal crown had been placed upon his head, his former powers were restored. But Solomon now knew that his kingdom, his wisdom, and his might would be taken from him if he did not use them properly.

Solomon then summoned the king of the Ammonites and asked him, "Why did you wish to kill the princess and the cook? They were innocent souls."

The Ammonite bowed and said, "Sire, I could not have killed the two. In a fit of foolish anger I sent them to the desert, and now I do not know what has become of them. I am saddened and I deeply regret my actions."

At once Solomon sent for Ne'amah. When she entered she bowed and kissed Solomon's hand. "Your daughter is my wife and I am your former cook," said Solomon. "May we rejoice in our blessings and may peace reign between our peoples." A great banquet was held and everyone joined in the joyous celebration.

The Talmud identifies Igrat as the "queen of demons."

The Ammonite city of Rabbath is known today as Amman, the capital of Jordan.

A Fortune for Chelm

Far away, somewhere in Eastern Europe, is the village of Chelm. The Chelmites are known far and wide for the foolish things they do and for the foolish things that happen to them. As they move from one folly to the next, they nevertheless maintain an optimistic attitude, and continue to follow the guidance of their Wise Men, whom they believe are without equal. This is the tale of one of the misadventures of the men of Chelm.

One day a stranger came upon the village of Chelm. As he walked through the streets he noticed the unusual way many of the Chelmites went about their business. They walked with their heads turned up, toward the sky. Growing more and more curious, the stranger sought out the Wise Men of Chelm. He wanted to find out why the people walked around in this strange way. The Wise Men were easy to recognize. They were very old, they wore long, black coats, black high hats, and had long, white beards. He asked the Wise Men why the people of the village walked as they did. The Wise Men invited the stranger to join them for tea, and told him this story.

Some time ago the Chelmites heard that a great fortune in gold awaited them in a far-off land. All they had to do to claim the fortune was to go to that distant land and bring it back to Chelm. Now, as one can imagine, the Chelmites were very excited about this treasure, and decided to send most of the village's men to retrieve the many bags of gold they hoped to find. To make sure that nothing went wrong along the way, they also asked their Wise Men to accompany the men.

Excitement grew as the Chelmites planned their

extraordinary journey. They were certain that once the fortune was brought back to Chelm, the people of the village would have no more problems. Everyone would have enough to eat, fine new clothes to wear, and big, luxurious houses to live in.

After much planning, the time for their journey had finally come. They walked hour after hour, until the day turned into night and night turned into another day. Day after day they traveled up steep mountains, down into dry deserts, and through green fields. At long last they arrived, and what they saw filled them with wonder. They stood, open-mouthed, staring at bags and bags of gold covering the countryside as far as the eye could see. They jumped for joy and congratulated themselves. There was their fortune, just as had been foretold!

They sang and danced, and envisioned the heroic welcome they would receive upon their return to Chelm. Their spirits soared as they lifted the bags of gold and threw them over their shoulders.

"The mayor will greet us with honors," one said.

"All the villagers will be proud," added another as he lifted more bags of gold onto his back.

The men had loaded so much gold onto their backs that they could hardly move. But their heads were filled with dreams of glory and the bags felt good. So, struggling and swaying under the tremendous weight of the gold, they began their journey home.

As the Chelmites walked hour after hour in the hot sun, the gold seemed to get heavier and heavier. Some men, with their legs bent by the weight of the heavy bags, could go no farther and stopped. They pleaded with their Wise Men, "Help! You must do something."

"Yes, yes. We must do something," agreed the Wise Men. They wrung their hands, paced back and forth,

Source ~ "A Fortune for Chelm" is a folk legend of the early part of the nineteenth century from Eastern Europe.

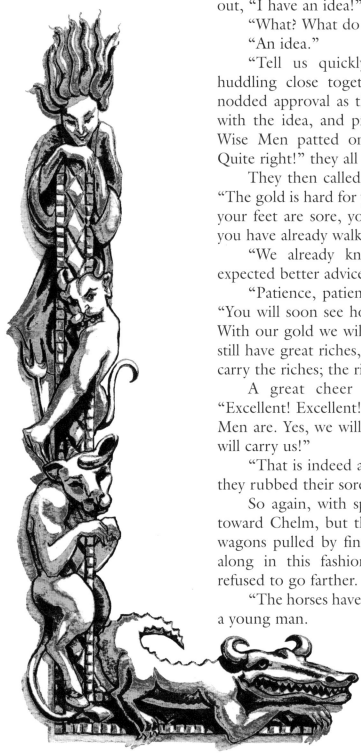

and concentrated. Sure enough, one of them soon cried out, "I have an idea!"

"What? What do you have?" they asked.

"An idea."

"Tell us quickly!" said the other Wise Men, huddling close together. They listened carefully and nodded approval as the plan was presented. Delighted with the idea, and proud of their good thinking, the Wise Men patted one another's back. "Quite right! Quite right!" they all agreed.

They then called the Chelmites together and said, "The gold is hard for you to carry because you are tired, your feet are sore, your backs have become weak, and you have already walked a long way."

"We already know that!" they protested. "We expected better advice from our Wise Men."

"Patience, patience," said the Wise Men, smiling. "You will soon see how wise we are. Here is our plan. With our gold we will buy horses and wagons. We will still have great riches, you see, but you will not have to carry the riches; the riches will carry you!"

A great cheer went up from the Chelmites. "Excellent! Excellent!" they cried. "How wise our Wise Men are. Yes, we will sit in our wagons and the horses will carry us!"

"That is indeed a wise idea," agreed all the men as they rubbed their sore and tired feet.

So again, with spirits high, the Chelmites set out toward Chelm, but this time they rode in new, sturdy wagons pulled by fine, strong horses. They continued along in this fashion until the horses stopped and refused to go farther.

"The horses haven't been given food or water," said a young man.

"Of course, horses must eat and drink. We just never thought of that. But we have no money for food."

Again the Chelmites appealed to their Wise Men. "Our horses have no food and water and will surely die if we don't do something quickly. What shall we do?"

A Chelmite, thinking without the aid of the Wise Men, cried out, "We can sell our horses to buy food because food, of course, is always valuable."

"How can you be so stupid!" shouted the Wise Men. "That is a very foolish idea! Our horses and wagons are so valuable that they are worth mountains and mountains of food. If we buy food it would be heavier than the gold. You could not carry the gold. How do you think you will carry a mountain of food? And, remember, food spoils; gold does not. No, no, we must not exchange our horses and wagons for food. Let us think of something that is light."

Again, the Wise Men wrung their hands, paced back and forth, and concentrated. After some time, the wisest of the Wise Men shouted out, "I have an idea!"

The others gathered around him, "Yes, yes, what is it?" they urged.

"You want something light?"

"Of course!" they answered.

"Feathers!"

"Feathers!" cried the Chelmites. "Of course, what could be lighter than a feather? Why didn't we think of that before?" And they praised the Wise Men, "Our Wise Men, they are truly wise."

And so the Chelmites sold their horses and wagons, and bought bags and bags of feathers that now covered the countryside as far as the eye could see.

The Chelmites shook their heads in despair. " Oh, my! How can we carry such great mounds of feathers?"

In eastern Poland there is a town named Chelm, and two smaller towns, Chelmno and Chelmza. Any one of these may have been the village of Chelm from which the fabled folkloric Chelm story collection originated.

And again they called upon their Wise Men to advise them.

The Wise Men huddled together. One of them wet his finger and stuck it up in the air. There was a strong wind blowing. At last the Wise Men announced to the Chelmites, "There is no need to worry. You have made a good trade. The feathers are better than horses."

"But what can you mean?" asked the Chelmites. "We don't understand."

"Of course you don't understand. How can you? You are not Wise Men. Now, do you know in what direction the wind is blowing?"

"Yes," said the Chelmites as they pointed toward the east.

Then, one of the Wise Men ripped open a bag of feathers and watched as they were quickly carried away by the wind.

"And in what direction are the feathers blowing?"

"East," they all shouted in delight. "Toward Chelm!"

"You are quite right," said the Wise Men smiling. "Now do you understand? My good people of Chelm, you do not have to carry the feathers home; God's own good wind will carry them!"

The Chelmites rejoiced with the Wise Men and sang out, "We understand! We understand!"

Then the men ripped open the many hundreds of bags filled with feathers, and soon the sky was black with feathers.

"Oh, how wonderful and wise our Wise Men are!" the men said as they watched the feathers fly away. "These feathers will fill the streets and roofs of Chelm. And we all know how valuable feathers are."

The Chelmites then resumed their long journey

home. When they arrived in Chelm, they found the village looking exactly as it had before they left. There were no feathers to be seen anywhere. They walked all around the town asking over and over, "Where are the feathers? What has happened to the feathers?"

"What are you talking about?" answered the villagers. "There are no feathers here."

"Oh no, we are ruined! We have lost everything!"

When the people of Chelm were told what had happened they joined in the lament. Everyone cried, "Our gold is gone, our horses and wagons are gone, our feathers are gone. We are ruined!"

The Wise Men stepped forward and raised their hands. "Stop," they demanded, "This is nonsense. Stop immediately!"

When the Chelmites had calmed down, the Wise Men continued, "Don't despair, dear Chelmites. The feathers will return in good time. Patience is what is called for. We need to wait patiently and have faith that our day will come. One day the sky will be black with feathers. When they fall on Chelm they will fill the town and from then on our lives will be filled with riches."

"And that is why the Chelmites walk around with their faces turned up," the Wise Men said to the stranger. "They are patient and hopeful that their day of great fortune will come. Actually, they are sure that their fortune will come. It is just a matter of time."

The stranger could see for himself that this hope kept the Chelmites in good spirits. He thanked the Wise Men for the tea and for the tale and went on his way, looking toward the heavens.

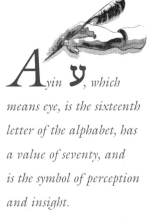

A*yin* ע, *which means eye, is the sixteenth letter of the alphabet, has a value of seventy, and is the symbol of perception and insight.*

The Flaw on the Diamond

Long ago, there was a rich and powerful king who was known the world over for his magnificent collection of jewels. The prize jewel in the collection was an exquisite diamond, the king's favorite possession. No finer stone existed anywhere in the world. One day, the king's jeweler stumbled as he was putting the diamond back in its case after cleaning it. The diamond fell and hit the ground so hard that it got a deep and ugly scratch. The king summoned to his castle the finest gem cutters and polishers in the kingdom to advise him how to repair the damaged stone. Each lapidary held the diamond up to the light and examined it carefully, and each came to the same conclusion: The stone could be polished, but the imperfection caused by the accident could never be removed.

The king listened to their views, then sent for the greatest lapidary in the world. The king challenged the great artist to not only repair the stone, but to make it more beautiful than it had been before.

The great lapidary carefully turned the diamond over and over in his hands. He accepted the king's awesome challenge, and immediately started his work on the stone. With great artistic skill, using the imperfection as the center, he engraved a delicate rosebud; around it he engraved rose petals; then out of the deep scratch he created a stem. He then brought the finished diamond to the king. When the king and all the other lapidaries saw the diamond with the beautiful rosebud, they were filled with amazement and with admiration for the master. Never before had the diamond been quite as beautiful, or as valuable. The king thanked the great lapidary most graciously, and sent him home with many treasures.

Source ~ "The Flaw on the Diamond" is a Midrash parable from eighteenth-century Eastern Europe.

"With perseverance a man can transform his worst fault into a virtue."

— FOX FABLES

God commanded Bezaleel, the craftsman "who cuts and sets stones," to fashion artifacts for the tabernacle in the wilderness.

— EXODUS 31:2-5

The Wise Maiden

Once, long ago there was a rich and mighty king who lived in a beautiful castle. He had a large harem of wives, mistresses, and servants who saw to his every need. The king had only one problem — he was haunted by a terrible dream, night after night.

In the dream, he saw a large ape wrapping his hairy arms around each of the king's wives and mistresses. Every morning the king was distressed, wondering what this dream could mean.

One morning he awoke especially downhearted. He thought gloomily, "Could the dream mean that an enemy is going to conquer my country and take all my wives?"

"What makes you so sad?" asked the chamberlain when he entered the king's chamber. "It is plain to see that you are greatly troubled. Tell me what disturbs you. Perhaps I shall be able to help."

"There is a dream…a terrible dream that I have over and over again," the king sighed. "I feel a grave disaster is about to befall me. Do you, by chance, know of anyone who can interpret dreams?"

"Sire," replied the chamberlain, "I have heard that three days' journey from here there is a wise maiden who can interpret the most confusing of dreams. If you wish, I could seek her out on your behalf."

"Yes, find this wise one and help me find the solution to this puzzle," said the king. Then he told the chamberlain the details of his dream. On that very morning the chamberlain left on the king's errand.

After the chamberlain had been traveling for three days, he came upon a farmer riding in his cart. "Peace be with you," said the chamberlain as he directed his mule

Source ~ "The Wise Maiden" is a wisdom riddle tale that dates from thirteenth-century Spain.

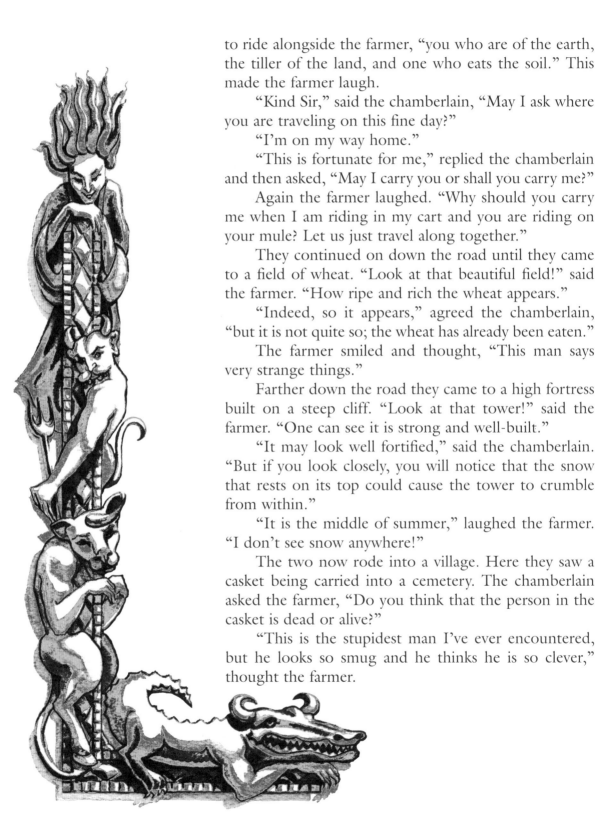

to ride alongside the farmer, "you who are of the earth, the tiller of the land, and one who eats the soil." This made the farmer laugh.

"Kind Sir," said the chamberlain, "May I ask where you are traveling on this fine day?"

"I'm on my way home."

"This is fortunate for me," replied the chamberlain and then asked, "May I carry you or shall you carry me?"

Again the farmer laughed. "Why should you carry me when I am riding in my cart and you are riding on your mule? Let us just travel along together."

They continued on down the road until they came to a field of wheat. "Look at that beautiful field!" said the farmer. "How ripe and rich the wheat appears."

"Indeed, so it appears," agreed the chamberlain, "but it is not quite so; the wheat has already been eaten."

The farmer smiled and thought, "This man says very strange things."

Farther down the road they came to a high fortress built on a steep cliff. "Look at that tower!" said the farmer. "One can see it is strong and well-built."

"It may look well fortified," said the chamberlain. "But if you look closely, you will notice that the snow that rests on its top could cause the tower to crumble from within."

"It is the middle of summer," laughed the farmer. "I don't see snow anywhere!"

The two now rode into a village. Here they saw a casket being carried into a cemetery. The chamberlain asked the farmer, "Do you think that the person in the casket is dead or alive?"

"This is the stupidest man I've ever encountered, but he looks so smug and he thinks he is so clever," thought the farmer.

"Farmer," said the chamberlain. "The sun has set and the hour grows late. Is there an inn nearby where we might find food and lodging?"

"I live not far from here. It would honor and please me to have you as a guest in my humble home. I can offer you food, and straw for your bed."

"Your hospitality is a kindness for which I am most grateful." He tipped his hat to the farmer and said, "Lead on, I shall follow you."

At the farmer's house the chamberlain was served food and drink. After supper the farmer led him to a loft where a bed of straw had been arranged, and bid him goodnight. The farmer then joined his wife and daughters at the hearth, where they sat warming themselves.

"Our guest is a simpleton! Listen to what he said on our journey today." Then the farmer repeated all the remarkable comments the chamberlain had made.

"Why do you call this man a fool, father?" asked the farmer's eldest daughter. "I think he is very wise. You have not understood him properly. Had you thought more carefully about the things he said, the meaning of his comments would have been revealed."

Startled, the farmer asked, "What, pray tell, could this man have possibly said that made any sense at all."

And the eldest daughter replied, "When he said 'you who are of the earth, the tiller of the land, and one who eats the soil,' he referred to the beginning of all food, which originally comes from the earth."

"When he asked you which one of you should carry the other, he wanted to know who would entertain the other. When one entertains a fellow traveler the journey is lightened, so one feels as if he is being carried."

"When he said the wheat has already been eaten, he meant that the owner of the field may have sold the crop

This story is adapted from a tale in "The Book of Delight" by Joseph ibn Zabara, the thirteenth-century Spanish-Jewish satirist and poet. The book contains tales, scientific discussions, and proverbs from the Middle Ages.

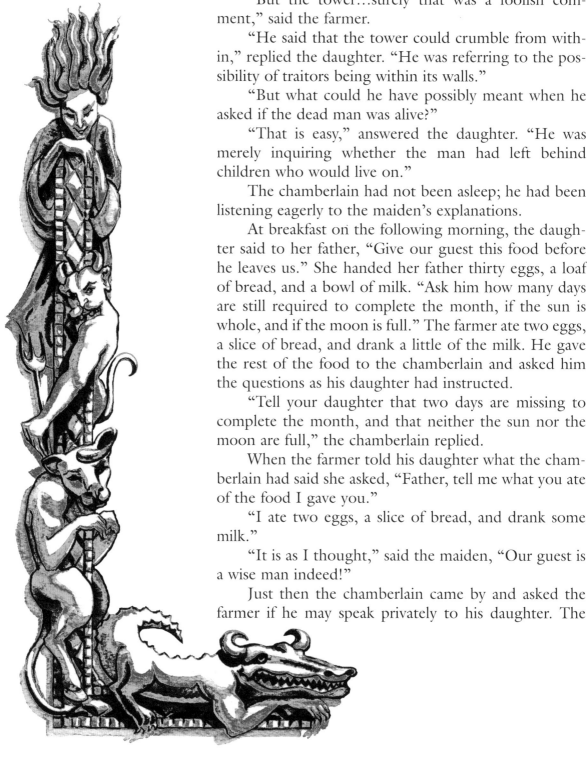

in advance of the harvest."

"But the tower...surely that was a foolish comment," said the farmer.

"He said that the tower could crumble from within," replied the daughter. "He was referring to the possibility of traitors being within its walls."

"But what could he have possibly meant when he asked if the dead man was alive?"

"That is easy," answered the daughter. "He was merely inquiring whether the man had left behind children who would live on."

The chamberlain had not been asleep; he had been listening eagerly to the maiden's explanations.

At breakfast on the following morning, the daughter said to her father, "Give our guest this food before he leaves us." She handed her father thirty eggs, a loaf of bread, and a bowl of milk. "Ask him how many days are still required to complete the month, if the sun is whole, and if the moon is full." The farmer ate two eggs, a slice of bread, and drank a little of the milk. He gave the rest of the food to the chamberlain and asked him the questions as his daughter had instructed.

"Tell your daughter that two days are missing to complete the month, and that neither the sun nor the moon are full," the chamberlain replied.

When the farmer told his daughter what the chamberlain had said she asked, "Father, tell me what you ate of the food I gave you."

"I ate two eggs, a slice of bread, and drank some milk."

"It is as I thought," said the maiden, "Our guest is a wise man indeed!"

Just then the chamberlain came by and asked the farmer if he may speak privately to his daughter. The

chamberlain told her the purpose of his journey and gave her the details of the king's dream.

When he had finished the maiden said, "I believe I understand what the dream signifies, but I must speak directly to the dreamer about its meaning."

The chamberlain then revealed his true identity to the farmer, and respectfully asked his permission to take his daughter to the palace to speak to the king. The farmer agreed. Shortly after their arrival at the palace, the chamberlain took the young maiden to meet the king in his private quarters. The king then repeated the details of his dream to her.

"Your Majesty, you must banish all worry from your mind!" said the young maiden. "The ape you see has no evil significance. But I hesitate to tell you the meaning of the dream because it is certain to cause you great distress."

The king said, "I command you to speak!"

"Yes, Sire. You need to search your harem thoroughly. Hidden among your wives, mistresses, and maidservants is a man disguised as a woman. He is the ape that haunts your dreams. He has caused some of your women to be unfaithful to you."

The astonished king ordered a search of the palace and grounds. It did not take long for the king's guards to find a young man masquerading as a woman — just as the young maiden had said.

The king sentenced the imposter to death, and banished all of his wives and mistresses from the palace.

Once order had been restored, the king asked the wise young maiden to be his bride. The people of the kingdom joined in their joyous celebration. As the king placed the royal crown upon his bride's head he swore to be faithful to her forever after.

Pei פ, the seventeenth letter of the alphabet has a value of eighty, and is the symbol of both speech and silence. The Talmud says it is sometimes a mitzvah to speak, and sometimes a mitzvah to be silent.

The Queen of Sheba tested King Solomon's wisdom by challenging him to solve riddles.

— 1 KINGS 10:1

Alexander
in Jerusalem

Long, long ago, when Alexander the Great ruled a
large part of the ancient world, the Jews of Jerusalem
refused to pay the taxes due him. They chose, instead, to

deposit the funds in their Temple, the House of God, thus steadily increasing their wealth and power. When Alexander learned of this, he was determined that the Jerusalem Jews be made to obey his laws. "If I cannot make the Jews heed my decrees, my own honor is worthless," said the King. And so it was that Alexander traveled to Palestine accompanied by his mighty army.

After a trek of twenty-six days, Alexander and his troops arrived in the city of Dan. From there he sent a letter to Jerusalem, addressed to The Jews of Jerusalem:

> By not paying your taxes for more than one year, you have refused to serve me. I now demand that these taxes be paid immediately. You must gather all the treasures you have collected in your House of God and turn them over to my emissaries.

The Jews of Jerusalem were distraught. They prayed to the Lord, dressed in sackcloth, and proclaimed a fast. The elders and sages formed a council to decide how to meet the Macedonian King's demands. The High Priest Anani was chosen to send a letter of reply to King Alexander:

Source ~ "Alexander in Jerusalem" is a historic legend from ancient Palestine, possibly from the third century B.C.E.

> Sire, that which you require from us is beyond our power to give. It is not within our authority to remove the treasures from the House of God. Our forefathers dedicated them to the needs of our widows, our orphans, our weak and our crippled, to sustain and strengthen them. We cannot, therefore, do as you command. If you so desire, we can send you one golden dinar from every Jewish household in Jerusalem, but we are not permitted to give you the treasures of our Temple.

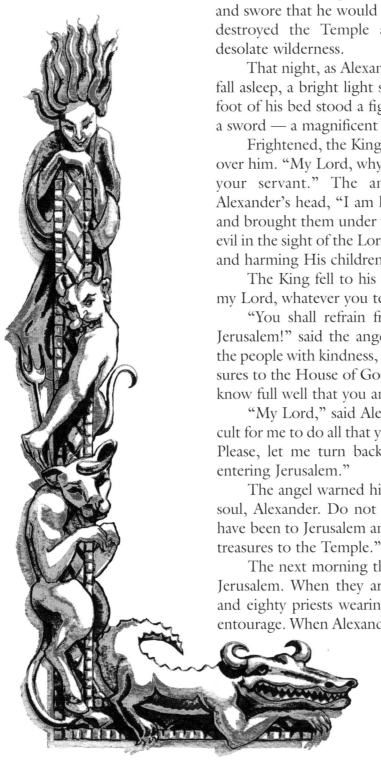

This letter angered King Alexander. He tore it up and swore that he would not leave Palestine until he had destroyed the Temple and turned Jerusalem into a desolate wilderness.

That night, as Alexander was in his bed and about to fall asleep, a bright light suddenly filled his room. At the foot of his bed stood a figure in white linens brandishing a sword — a magnificent angel of the Lord.

Frightened, the King addressed the angel as he stood over him. "My Lord, why do you wish to strike me? I am your servant." The angel swung the sword over Alexander's head, "I am he who has subdued the people and brought them under your rule. Now you swear to do evil in the sight of the Lord by laying His country to waste and harming His children."

The King fell to his knees and pleaded. "I beg you, my Lord, whatever you tell me I shall do."

"You shall refrain from doing evil to the Jews of Jerusalem!" said the angel. "You must seek peace, treat the people with kindness, and give some of your own treasures to the House of God. If you disobey my command, know full well that you and all that is yours shall perish!"

"My Lord," said Alexander, "It would be very difficult for me to do all that you say without losing my honor. Please, let me turn back. I shall return home without entering Jerusalem."

The angel warned him again, "Beware for your very soul, Alexander. Do not return to your home until you have been to Jerusalem and have given some of your own treasures to the Temple."

The next morning the King and his army set out to Jerusalem. When they arrived at the city's gates, Anani and eighty priests wearing holy robes received the royal entourage. When Alexander saw Anani he dismounted his

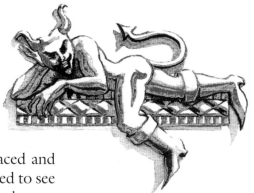

horse, fell to the ground before him, and embraced and kissed his feet. Alexander's warriors were astonished to see this. "What are you doing?" they asked. "Why do you degrade yourself with this old man? All the kings of the world bow before you, yet you hold your own honor in such low esteem that you have prostrated yourself before this man! What will the people of the world say now?"

"This old man has the likeness of the Angel of God who goes before me in times of war. He is the one who conquers the people and causes them to bow to me. This is why I show him my deepest respect."

When the High Priest Anani heard the King's words, he prostrated himself before the God of Israel. After he had blessed the Lord aloud he said to the King, "If you have found the sight of me favorable, please do no evil unto the people of Jerusalem. They are your servants."

"I have vowed to do no evil unto your people," said Alexander. "It is you who must command the Jews of Jerusalem to do no injury unto us."

Then the priests and the city elders escorted the King and his warriors into Jerusalem, where they rested for several days. On the fourth day Alexander said to Anani, "Please show me the House of the great God whose people honor me." Anani was happy to grant his request and accompanied the King and his men to God's Temple. When Alexander entered, he saw before him the same angel dressed in white linens. He flung himself to the ground and lay still before him. When Alexander finally spoke, his voice rang out, "This is the House of God whose equal is not to be found in all the world. I command that vessels of silver, gold, and precious jewels be brought forth from my treasury. I ask that they be added to the treasury of the House of God."

And all the people of Jerusalem rejoiced!

Alexander the Great ascended the Macedonian throne in 336 B.C.E. During his thirteen-year reign, Alexander conquered a great part of the ancient world uniting the East and the West. He is said to have cherished the idea of creating a "world brotherhood of all men."

The Prophet Elijah Saves the Baal Shem Tov

The Prophet Elijah is the source of more Jewish and medieval folklore than any other Biblical hero. Legend tells us that, because he is partly human and partly divine, he is especially tolerant of our human failings. As a counselor and protector of all people in times of trouble, he is portrayed as a devoted shepherd watching over his flock, always ready to help a sheep who has gone astray. Stories abound of his helping the poor and comforting the sorrowful. Many tell of Elijah himself going before God to plead a person's case.

The Bible suggests that the Prophet Elijah did not die like other mortals but was "translated" to heaven while he was still alive. One day, as he was walking with a disciple, he was swept up in a whirlwind, placed in a chariot of fire, and taken to heaven (II Kings 2:11). Legend tells us that in heaven Elijah stands between paradise and hell, and acts as an escort for all souls. He leads the repentant to paradise, and escorts the sinners out of hell on one day each week for Sabbath, their day of rest, and then returns them when it is over.

As an angel of the highest rank, Elijah moves among the people of the earth in time, space, and eternity, and takes on human shape to accomplish his important tasks. His disguises allow him to do good deeds without being recognized. Then after he has gone, and only then, his true identity is revealed.

*S*ource ~"The Prophet Elijah Saves the Baal Shem Tov" is a Hasidic legend that dates from eighteenth-century Eastern Europe.

An angel visited Elijah as he sat under a juniper tree.

—1 KINGS 19:5

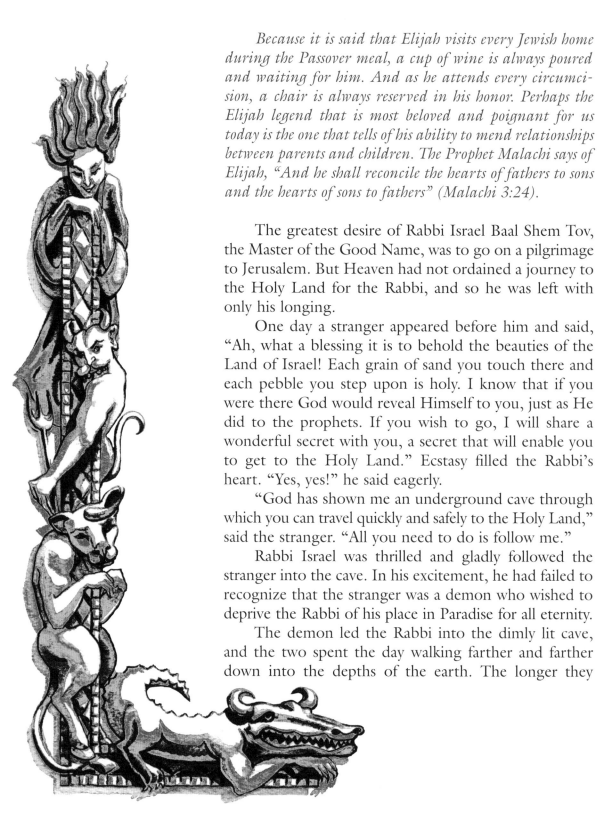

Because it is said that Elijah visits every Jewish home during the Passover meal, a cup of wine is always poured and waiting for him. And as he attends every circumcision, a chair is always reserved in his honor. Perhaps the Elijah legend that is most beloved and poignant for us today is the one that tells of his ability to mend relationships between parents and children. The Prophet Malachi says of Elijah, "And he shall reconcile the hearts of fathers to sons and the hearts of sons to fathers" (Malachi 3:24).

The greatest desire of Rabbi Israel Baal Shem Tov, the Master of the Good Name, was to go on a pilgrimage to Jerusalem. But Heaven had not ordained a journey to the Holy Land for the Rabbi, and so he was left with only his longing.

One day a stranger appeared before him and said, "Ah, what a blessing it is to behold the beauties of the Land of Israel! Each grain of sand you touch there and each pebble you step upon is holy. I know that if you were there God would reveal Himself to you, just as He did to the prophets. If you wish to go, I will share a wonderful secret with you, a secret that will enable you to get to the Holy Land." Ecstasy filled the Rabbi's heart. "Yes, yes!" he said eagerly.

"God has shown me an underground cave through which you can travel quickly and safely to the Holy Land," said the stranger. "All you need to do is follow me."

Rabbi Israel was thrilled and gladly followed the stranger into the cave. In his excitement, he had failed to recognize that the stranger was a demon who wished to deprive the Rabbi of his place in Paradise for all eternity.

The demon led the Rabbi into the dimly lit cave, and the two spent the day walking farther and farther down into the depths of the earth. The longer they

walked, the darker and damper the cave became.

Tired and out of breath, Rabbi Israel finally asked, "How much farther is it? I think I had better rest awhile before going on."

"You must take heart, Rabbi," answered the demon. "Very soon we shall be in the Land of Israel. All we need to do is walk across the log. . .over here."

As he said this, he stepped onto the log, which was placed across a bed of quicksand. He then turned and motioned for Rabbi Israel to follow. The demon raised his arms, ready to push the rabbi into the deadly quicksand. "Keep coming, Rabbi, you're almost there! Just one more step."

The Rabbi, struggling close behind him, raised his foot to step upon the log. Just then, the Prophet Elijah appeared in a blaze of brilliant light. Swiftly, he grabbed the Rabbi and led him back to safety.

In that very instant, Rabbi Israel understood that his guide was a demon whose intent was evil. He cast a spell upon the wicked demon, a spell that sent him running away, screaming in terror!

Elijah then led Baal Shem Tov out of the cave and returned him safely to his home. From that day forth the Rabbi was very careful not let his enthusiasm and excitement cloud his better judgment.

The Baal Shem Tov, "Master of the Good Name," was born Israel ben Eliezer in a small Ukrainian village about 1700. He was the charismatic founder, in the mid-eighteenth century, of the Jewish sect of Hasidism. He said that laughter, song, and dance, are the highest forms of prayer. He is revered today in the Hasidic movement worldwide.

The Story of Ruth

Long ago, in the ancient land of Moab, a young girl sat beside the Sea of Salt watching the sun set over the western hills. She was grateful for the soft breeze that blew across her face and cooled her in the summer heat. Her friends had gone to tend the goats, and she was glad to have this moment alone, to gaze across the crystal waters, and dream about her future. On that day Ruth could not have imagined the life that was before her, but she did sense that her life would change. Indeed, she would have an extraordinary life, a life very different from that of any other Moabite girl.

Ruth often felt like a stranger in her own land and found little in common with other girls her age. She did have one true friend, Na'arah, a slave girl Ruth's father had brought back from the land of Reuben in northern

Moab. Na'arah spoke with an accent and had odd customs; she did not eat meat, and on one day each week she refused to work, even when beaten for her refusal. Ruth was impressed by the way Na'arah honored her beliefs and traditions. She loved to spend time talking with her, and thought that this poor slave girl was the best and wisest person she knew.

Ruth listened for hours as Na'arah told stories of her home, her people, and of her god. It was hard for Ruth to understand this god whom no one could see. He was not made of stone or gold. You couldn't find him anywhere; yet Na'arah said that he was everywhere! He did not permit his people to have other gods, and he determined for his people what was right and what was wrong. Again and again, Ruth found herself drawn to Na'arah's stories about her god. They made her feel less strange, less different. One day Ruth's father sent Na'arah back home to her own people. Ruth felt lost and lonely for a very long time — until the people from Judah came to Moab.

Among the Judaeans was an elderly couple who came with their grown sons. Most Moabites, including Ruth's family, respected this family because they had been rich and honored in their own country. They came with money, bought land, and built a large house. They did not take part in the Moabite festivals and had customs that many Moabites considered odd. This made some people dislike them. But Ruth understood this family and, through her friendship with Na'arah, was already familiar with their customs. She loved to visit the family, often accompanied by her friend Orpah. Elimelech, the head of this Judaean family, felt that his sons were spending too much time with the Moabite girls, but his wife, Naomi, liked them and spent many

Source ~ "The Story of Ruth" is a Biblical legend based on the Book of Ruth.

One biblical meaning of Ruth is "friendship."

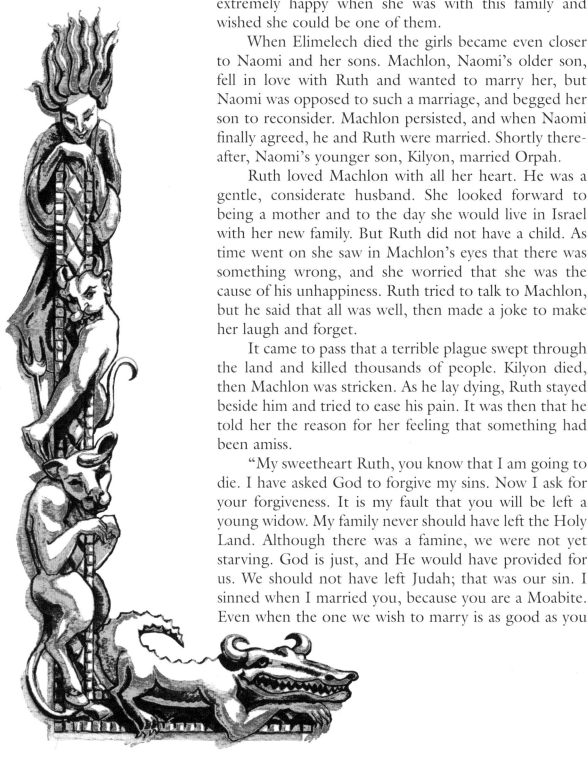

hours teaching them to cook and sew. Ruth was extremely happy when she was with this family and wished she could be one of them.

When Elimelech died the girls became even closer to Naomi and her sons. Machlon, Naomi's older son, fell in love with Ruth and wanted to marry her, but Naomi was opposed to such a marriage, and begged her son to reconsider. Machlon persisted, and when Naomi finally agreed, he and Ruth were married. Shortly thereafter, Naomi's younger son, Kilyon, married Orpah.

Ruth loved Machlon with all her heart. He was a gentle, considerate husband. She looked forward to being a mother and to the day she would live in Israel with her new family. But Ruth did not have a child. As time went on she saw in Machlon's eyes that there was something wrong, and she worried that she was the cause of his unhappiness. Ruth tried to talk to Machlon, but he said that all was well, then made a joke to make her laugh and forget.

It came to pass that a terrible plague swept through the land and killed thousands of people. Kilyon died, then Machlon was stricken. As he lay dying, Ruth stayed beside him and tried to ease his pain. It was then that he told her the reason for her feeling that something had been amiss.

"My sweetheart Ruth, you know that I am going to die. I have asked God to forgive my sins. Now I ask for your forgiveness. It is my fault that you will be left a young widow. My family never should have left the Holy Land. Although there was a famine, we were not yet starving. God is just, and He would have provided for us. We should not have left Judah; that was our sin. I sinned when I married you, because you are a Moabite. Even when the one we wish to marry is as good as you

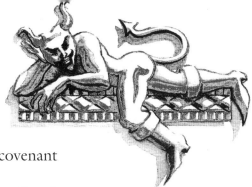

are, we must marry only those who are of the covenant of God."

"Oh, my dearest Machlon! Why didn't you tell me? I would have gladly come into your covenant."

"It would not have been right for you to join our covenant just so that we may marry. I pray that God, who knows your heart and does not punish the innocent, will bless you and make up for any suffering I have caused you." Ruth wept and held him close. When Machlon died her heart was broken.

Naomi, whose name means "pleasant one," was so overcome by the loss of her two sons that she changed her name to Marah, "bitter one." She wept night and day. And she prayed. She begged God to forgive her and her family their sins. Her only wish was to return to her home in Israel, to die on holy soil.

Ruth wanted to go with her mother-in-law. She said she would rather be a stranger in Israel than at home in Moab, but wondered if she would be allowed to enter Israel. She remembered Machlon's words, "...because you are a Moabite." What did he mean?

"Mother, is it true that Moabites cannot become Israelites?" she asked.

"Anyone who is completely sincere can come into the covenant," said Naomi, "but Moabites cannot marry Israelites. That is why I did not want my sons to marry here. If they had listened to me, they might still be alive, and you and Orpah would be happy with Moabite husbands and children." And Naomi wept.

Ruth gently took hold of Naomi. "Listen to me, Mother, you must not pity me. I shall never marry a Moabite. I want to stay with you. If you go home, I shall go with you and join the faith of Israel, even if I never marry again."

Tzaddi צ, the eighteenth letter of the alphabet, has a value of ninety and is the symbol of righteousness. This letter is commonly called tzaddik, like the righteous and devout holy men.

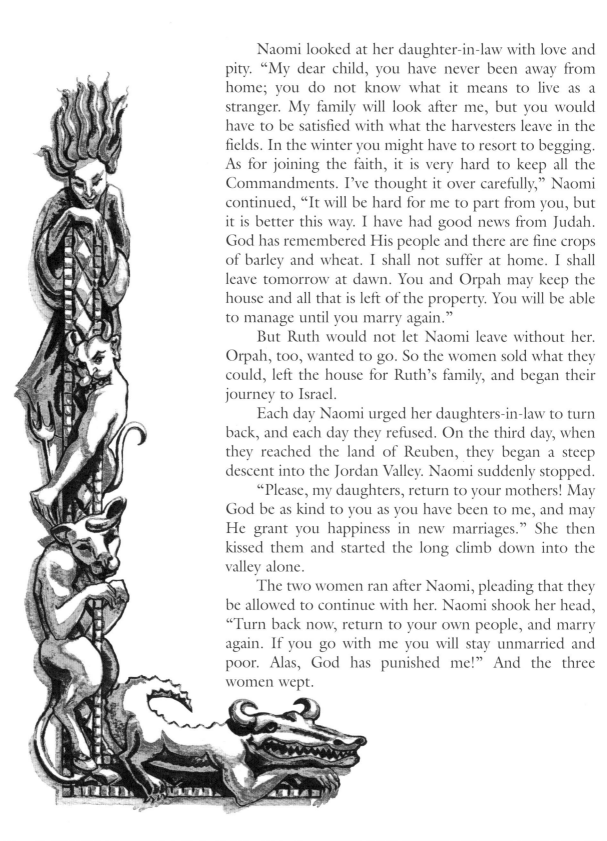

Naomi looked at her daughter-in-law with love and pity. "My dear child, you have never been away from home; you do not know what it means to live as a stranger. My family will look after me, but you would have to be satisfied with what the harvesters leave in the fields. In the winter you might have to resort to begging. As for joining the faith, it is very hard to keep all the Commandments. I've thought it over carefully," Naomi continued, "It will be hard for me to part from you, but it is better this way. I have had good news from Judah. God has remembered His people and there are fine crops of barley and wheat. I shall not suffer at home. I shall leave tomorrow at dawn. You and Orpah may keep the house and all that is left of the property. You will be able to manage until you marry again."

But Ruth would not let Naomi leave without her. Orpah, too, wanted to go. So the women sold what they could, left the house for Ruth's family, and began their journey to Israel.

Each day Naomi urged her daughters-in-law to turn back, and each day they refused. On the third day, when they reached the land of Reuben, they began a steep descent into the Jordan Valley. Naomi suddenly stopped.

"Please, my daughters, return to your mothers! May God be as kind to you as you have been to me, and may He grant you happiness in new marriages." She then kissed them and started the long climb down into the valley alone.

The two women ran after Naomi, pleading that they be allowed to continue with her. Naomi shook her head, "Turn back now, return to your own people, and marry again. If you go with me you will stay unmarried and poor. Alas, God has punished me!" And the three women wept.

Orpah finally gave up. She kissed Naomi and turned back toward Moab, but Ruth stayed at Naomi's side.

Naomi took Ruth by the shoulders and, looking steadily into her eyes, said, "Ruth, there goes your sister-in-law, back to her people, you must go with her!"

But Ruth steadfastly refused to leave Naomi. "Where you go, I will go; where you sleep, I will sleep; where you die, I will die. Your people are my people; your God is my God. I swear by the God of Israel that only death shall separate me from you!"

Naomi said no more. She now saw that Ruth's desire to join her covenant was most sincere.

When Naomi and Ruth reached Bethlehem, Ruth appeared before the elders to declare her faith. She immersed herself in the *mikvah*, "ritual bath," and thereafter offered a sacrifice upon the altar.

It was the barley season in Bethlehem, and Naomi and Ruth found a small but comfortable cottage near the fields. There, the two women settled into a modest and peaceful life. Each day Ruth went out into the fields for the grain left behind by the harvesters. Bo'az, the owner of the fields, soon noticed her and made her acquaintance. Bo'az was attracted to Ruth's courage, her willingness to work hard, and to the care she bestowed upon her mother-in-law. He grew to love her and one day asked for her hand in marriage. Ruth wanted to marry Bo'az, but not without the approval of the elders. Bo'az consulted the elders and the elders consulted the prophets. The prophets said that within the true tradition of marriage, they saw no reason why a Moabite woman, who had joined the covenant, should not marry a man of Israel.

And so it was that Ruth and Bo'az married. They had a son called Oved, who had a son called Yishai, whose son was David, King of Israel.

Ancient Moab today is part of Jordan.

Kuf **ק**, *the nineteenth letter of the alphabet, has a value of 100, and is the symbol of holiness and growth cycles as expressed in nature.*

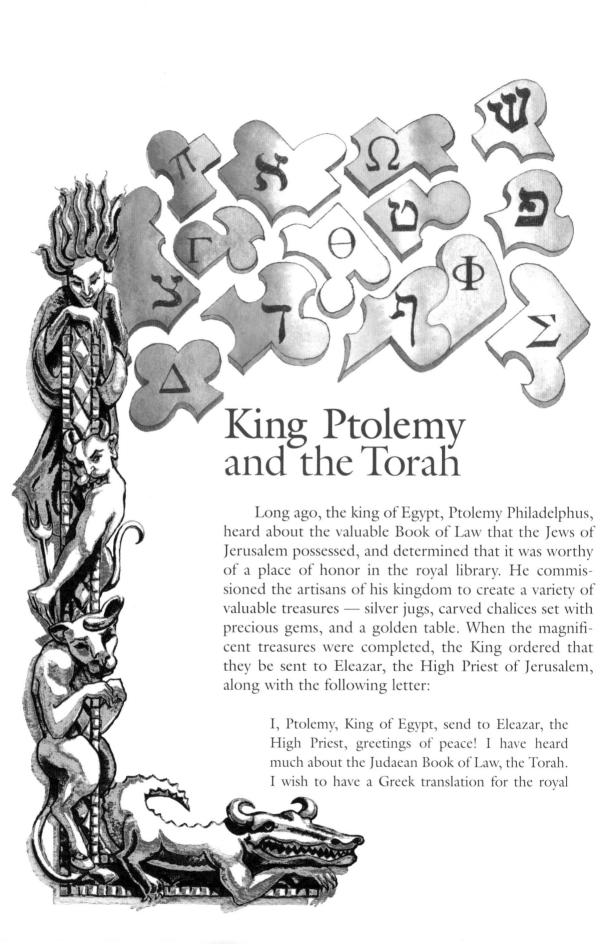

King Ptolemy and the Torah

Long ago, the king of Egypt, Ptolemy Philadelphus, heard about the valuable Book of Law that the Jews of Jerusalem possessed, and determined that it was worthy of a place of honor in the royal library. He commissioned the artisans of his kingdom to create a variety of valuable treasures — silver jugs, carved chalices set with precious gems, and a golden table. When the magnificent treasures were completed, the King ordered that they be sent to Eleazar, the High Priest of Jerusalem, along with the following letter:

> I, Ptolemy, King of Egypt, send to Eleazar, the High Priest, greetings of peace! I have heard much about the Judaean Book of Law, the Torah. I wish to have a Greek translation for the royal

library. I appeal to you to send to Egypt your wisest scholars in order to accomplish this. My sincerest gratitude is expressed with the gifts presented to you by my servant Aristeas.

Eleazar read the letter and was filled with joy. He was happy that the Torah had so impressed the Egyptian King. He accepted the gifts and said to Aristeas, "Please remain here for several days as our guest while I choose those who will return with you to Egypt."

From each of the twelve tribes of Israel, Eleazar selected six scholars. When the seventy-two sages were gathered, ready to leave for Egypt, he said to Aristeas, "Please do not let the King detain them after their work is done. If I did not consider the blessings that the Torah can bring, I would not permit these sages to depart from here. My soul hangs on their souls, and it is only with great reluctance that we part one from the other."

The sages and Aristeas bid the High Priest farewell and set out on their journey. Upon their arrival in Alexandria, the Judaean wise men went to the King and greeted him with their blessings, and those of Eleazar.

"Do you have the Torah scroll?" asked the King.

"Here it is," they answered, as they carefully removed it from a chest and unrolled it for the King.

Ptolemy regarded the scroll with awe. He blessed the seventy-two sages, bowed before them seven times, and warmly clasped each man's hand.

"Today is a joyous day," said the King. "A feast has been arranged in your honor." He then led the sages into the great hall of the palace to one of several banquet tables. Seated at the other tables were the princes and all the great men of the kingdom who were there to celebrate the seventy-two guests of honor.

Source ~ "King Ptolemy and the Torah" is a historic legend from ancient Israel, possibly from the 2nd century B.C.E.

The sages' Greek translation of the Torah is called "Septuagint"

Before they sat down to eat, one of the sages offered a prayer, "Eternal Father, may you bless King Ptolemy, and may everything he undertakes meet with success. Bless also his wife, his children, and his subjects."

"Amen!" said the other wise men.

At the end of the meal the King put questions to the Jewish sages to test their wisdom:

"When can a king's rule be successful?"

"When he serves God, rewards the good, and punishes the wicked."

"How can a man increase his possessions?"

"By giving to the poor."

"How can a ruler triumph over his enemies?"

"By striving for peace and by relying on God more than on his army."

"When do we reveal our true strength of character?"

"In misfortune."

"How should a man behave when misfortune occurs?"

"He should pray to God, put his trust in Him and know that there is not a person on earth who has not at some time had misfortune."

"How can we remain truthful?"

"By reflecting upon how disgraceful lying is."

"What is the most difficult thing for a king?"

"To master himself."

"How can we silence those who slander us?"

"By doing good."

"Unto whom shall we do good?"

"First unto our parents and friends, and then unto all others."

"How can one who has been evil regain his honor?"

"By doing good again."

"Can one acquire righteousness through knowledge?"

"Indeed. The understanding person can distinguish

between good and evil."

"How can one guard oneself against anger?"

"By reflecting on its consequences."

"Which of our works will last forever?"

"Our righteous works will last forever."

"For whom shall man feel pity?"

"For those who experience great misfortune, because it is not always possible for us to help them."

"Why do so few people strive for wisdom?"

"Because most people regard riches as their highest goal. The wise, however, know that riches alone cannot bring happiness."

"What shall we do in days of good fortune?"

"We should think about what we already have and what we still wish to accomplish."

King Ptolemy was greatly satisfied with the wisdom of the sages. He thanked them and presented each with gifts of gold. He then had Aristeas escort them to an island where each, armed with his own copy of the Torah, was lodged in a separate house. Food, comfort and servant were provided to each sage. Ptolemy also instructed that the door to each house be locked as soon as work on the translation began. He did not want the sages to communicate with one another while they were translating. If all the versions of the Torah were alike, he would be sure that the translations were accurate. After seventy-two days the work was completed.

The sages gave King Ptolemy the seventy-two translations. After Ptolemy compared all versions, and found that they were exactly the same in every detail, he ordered the scrolls to be placed and preserved in the royal library.

The King then expressed his gratitude to the wise men, and sent them home laden with gifts.

King Ptolemy II of Egypt, known as Ptolemy Philadelphus, "brotherly," reigned from 285-246 B.C.E. During his reign, the Library of Alexandria grew to be the largest in the ancient world.

Reish ר, the twentieth letter of the alphabet, has a value of 200 and represents a person's ability to choose greatness over wrongdoing.

The Location of Paradise

Once, a long time ago, a famous *tzaddik*, a "righteous person," had a dream in which he was on a journey to Paradise. In this dream he walked for many miles until he came to a high mountain. As he started to climb the mountain, three angels suddenly appeared and stopped him from going farther. The angels told him that in order for him to enter Paradise he must go to the well of the Prophetess Miriam and immerse himself in the water.

The tzaddik agreed to do as the angels instructed and went directly to the well. He peered down into the dark, damp well, and became frightened when he saw how very deep the well was. Then the angels appeared once more and told him that they would help. They held him tightly, then gently immersed him in the water from head to toe. At that moment the tzaddik was transported straight to Paradise, with his angel guides at his side.

When he entered Paradise all he saw were a few saints reading books and studying Torah. This surprised the tzaddik, who asked the angels, "Why are there so few saints here? Can these few be all that are in Paradise?"

"Young man," the angels replied, "do you think that all the saints are in Paradise? This is not so, no, not at all. Paradise is in the saints!"

Source ~ "The Location of Paradise" is a Hasidic legend dating from eighteenth-century Eastern Europe.

Lamed-vav Tzaddikim is a term in Jewish tradition that refers to the group of thirty-six (the sum of the letters lamed and vav) "hidden saints" in every generation who are so righteous and just that their presence allows the world to continue to exist.

Rabbinical Math

Once there were three men who pooled their money in order to purchase horses. Altogether, they had enough money with which to purchase seventeen horses. One man had contributed about half of the money, the second man gave approximately a third of the money, and the third man's share was about one ninth. When the time came for them to divide the horses among them, they did not know how to do it fairly. So they decided to seek the advice of the rabbi. They went to his house, and told him of their dilemma.

"Let me sleep on the matter overnight," said the rabbi. "Return tomorrow morning and bring all the horses with you."

The three partners followed the rabbi's instructions and returned to his house the next morning with the horses. They waited eagerly for the rabbi's solution. After some time, the rabbi came out and walked directly over to his own stable. He brought out a horse, mounted it, and rode up to the men and their seventeen horses.

"Now, gentlemen," said the rabbi, "we have here eighteen horses. The partner who paid one half will take nine of them; The man who paid one third will take six horses; and last, the one whose share is one ninth is entitled to two horses. When you add these up, seventeen horses will have been distributed."

The rabbi then rode his own horse back to his stable and returned to his study of the Talmud.

Source ~ "Rabbinical Math" is an aggadah folktale from a Midrash.

Shin **שׁ**, *the twenty-first letter of the alphabet, has a value of 300, and is the symbol of divine power and script. The three parts of Shin represent the three primary colors - red, yellow, and blue, which blend to form the colors of the rainbow.*

The Orphan Boy Who Won the Bride

Once upon a time, long ago, in a tiny cottage on the estate of a great nobleman, lived a man and wife who longed for a child. They prayed to God for the blessing of a child but one never came. One day the man decided to seek the help of a rabbi. "Rabbi, my good wife and I want very much to have a child. We have prayed for many years but no child has come. Will you pray for us and ask the Lord to send us this blessing? If a child is born to us, we shall be grateful forever."

The rabbi agreed to help this couple, and prayed to God to bless them with a child. His prayers were answered with the birth of a beautiful son. The baby grew into a fine boy in the loving home of his adoring mother and father. But when the boy was five years old tragedy struck. Both the man and wife died suddenly, leaving the boy an orphan. When the nobleman heard this terrible news he took the boy into his home and raised him as his own son.

The nobleman provided a good home for the boy. He was a happy child who loved to play in the streams and forests of the nobleman's large estate. He ran and swam, built fortresses made of sand, and carved toys made of wood.

Source ~ "The Orphan Boy Who Won the Bride" is a folktale from Poland that dates from the middle of the nineteenth century.

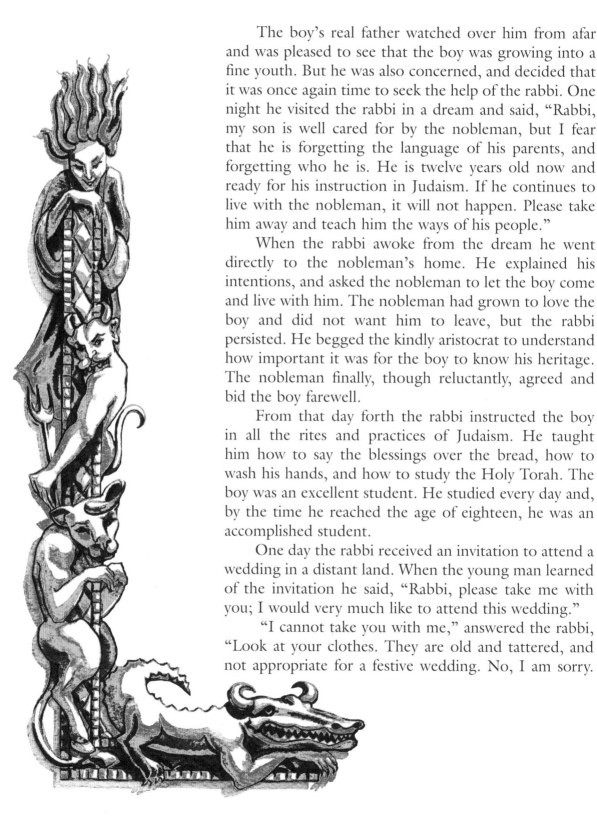

The boy's real father watched over him from afar and was pleased to see that the boy was growing into a fine youth. But he was also concerned, and decided that it was once again time to seek the help of the rabbi. One night he visited the rabbi in a dream and said, "Rabbi, my son is well cared for by the nobleman, but I fear that he is forgetting the language of his parents, and forgetting who he is. He is twelve years old now and ready for his instruction in Judaism. If he continues to live with the nobleman, it will not happen. Please take him away and teach him the ways of his people."

When the rabbi awoke from the dream he went directly to the nobleman's home. He explained his intentions, and asked the nobleman to let the boy come and live with him. The nobleman had grown to love the boy and did not want him to leave, but the rabbi persisted. He begged the kindly aristocrat to understand how important it was for the boy to know his heritage. The nobleman finally, though reluctantly, agreed and bid the boy farewell.

From that day forth the rabbi instructed the boy in all the rites and practices of Judaism. He taught him how to say the blessings over the bread, how to wash his hands, and how to study the Holy Torah. The boy was an excellent student. He studied every day and, by the time he reached the age of eighteen, he was an accomplished student.

One day the rabbi received an invitation to attend a wedding in a distant land. When the young man learned of the invitation he said, "Rabbi, please take me with you; I would very much like to attend this wedding."

"I cannot take you with me," answered the rabbi, "Look at your clothes. They are old and tattered, and not appropriate for a festive wedding. No, I am sorry.

You cannot join me for this occasion."

"I will get the right clothes when I get there," said the young man.

"Dear boy, I do not have enough money to take you with me," said the rabbi, "I barely have enough for myself. Now, let us have no more talk of this."

On the day of departure the young man accompanied the rabbi to the dock. The rabbi boarded the ship, waved goodbye to the youth, and went to his cabin. He did not know that just before the ship had pulled up its anchor, the young man had slipped aboard and had hidden among the crates in the cargo storage area.

When the ship reached the open sea a sudden storm arose. Giant waves tossed the ship about, forcing it farther and farther off course. When the storm finally passed, the ship was hopelessly lost, and was embedded in a block of frozen ice. Many days passed without the arrival of help, and the passengers and crew ran out of food. Then another violent storm broke the ship free from the ice and sent it careening across the ocean, where it finally came to rest near a small island.

The young man, along with many hungry passengers, jumped off the ship and swam to the island in search of food. They found an apple tree filled with fruit. The young man climbed the tree, ate some apples and threw some down for the others. Those who ate the fruit fell fast asleep.

The young man slept on the branches high up in the tree until a soft breeze awakened him. Startled, he looked around and saw that all the apples in the tree had turned to stones on which beautiful Hebrew letters appeared. He then saw that the passengers were no longer on the beach and that the ship was sailing away. He tried to make himself comfortable, settled down to

In mystical folklore secret incantations were often written on apples, citrons, and other foods that were eaten for the benefit their magical power. A pomegranate is said to contain 613 seeds, one for each of the 613 mitzvot listed in the Torah.

The Tree of Knowledge is a symbol of the Written Law, and the Tree of Life represents the Oral Law.

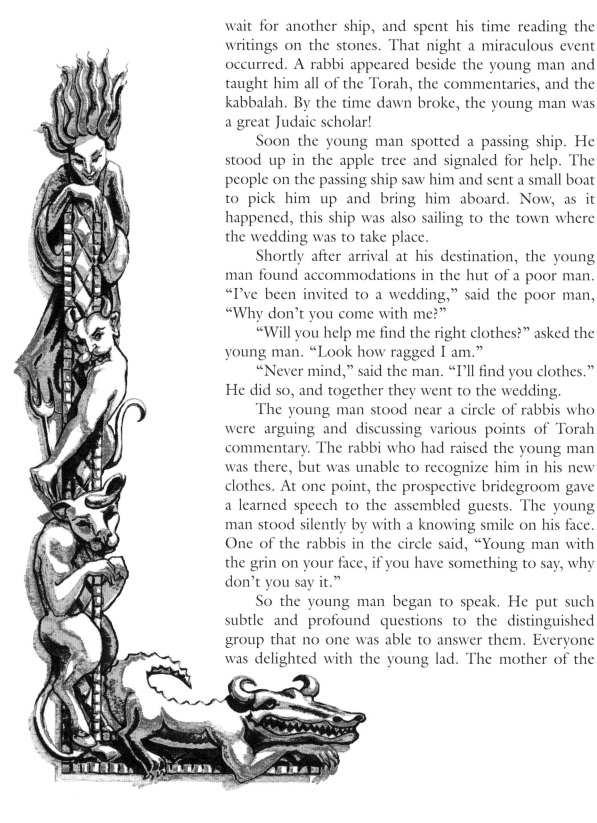

wait for another ship, and spent his time reading the writings on the stones. That night a miraculous event occurred. A rabbi appeared beside the young man and taught him all of the Torah, the commentaries, and the kabbalah. By the time dawn broke, the young man was a great Judaic scholar!

Soon the young man spotted a passing ship. He stood up in the apple tree and signaled for help. The people on the passing ship saw him and sent a small boat to pick him up and bring him aboard. Now, as it happened, this ship was also sailing to the town where the wedding was to take place.

Shortly after arrival at his destination, the young man found accommodations in the hut of a poor man. "I've been invited to a wedding," said the poor man, "Why don't you come with me?"

"Will you help me find the right clothes?" asked the young man. "Look how ragged I am."

"Never mind," said the man. "I'll find you clothes." He did so, and together they went to the wedding.

The young man stood near a circle of rabbis who were arguing and discussing various points of Torah commentary. The rabbi who had raised the young man was there, but was unable to recognize him in his new clothes. At one point, the prospective bridegroom gave a learned speech to the assembled guests. The young man stood silently by with a knowing smile on his face. One of the rabbis in the circle said, "Young man with the grin on your face, if you have something to say, why don't you say it."

So the young man began to speak. He put such subtle and profound questions to the distinguished group that no one was able to answer them. Everyone was delighted with the young lad. The mother of the

bride-to-be said to her husband, "Now that's the sort of husband our daughter should have."

"You're right!" replied her husband. They canceled the wedding on the spot and betrothed their daughter to the learned stranger.

The young man insisted that his wedding be celebrated in the poor man's hut.

"How can that be done?" asked the poor man. "My hut is such a tiny place."

"Never mind. Everyone will fit."

The wedding day soon arrived, and the hut was modestly, though nicely, decorated for the celebration. When the musicians came, the young man told them not to play until midnight. Meanwhile, people began to arrive; then more people arrived. It was amazing! No matter how many people were in the hut, there was always room for more. The hut grew larger and larger and larger until it accommodated all the people of the village.

Shortly before midnight the dark sky turned darker and a great gust of wind suddenly shook the hut. The young man ran outside. The rabbi who had raised the young man finally recognized him, and he ran outside. Then all of the wedding guests ran outside. The entire wedding party watched in awe as an enormous cloud descended from the heavens. When the cloud touched the ground the young man's father and mother stepped from it, followed by King David.

"Now play!" cried the young man to his musicians.

And they played, and the food was served, and there was dancing, and I too was there and had a good little glass of brandy, in honor of the beautiful bride and the scholarly groom.

In Jewish weddings the marriage ceremony is performed beneath a canopy called a "chupah."

———————

"My beloved is mine, and I am his" is traditionally said by the bride to the groom.
— SONG OF SOLOMON 2:16

———————

All the guests at a wedding wish the bride and groom joyous Good Luck, in Hebrew "mazel tov!"

Moses Receives the Word of God

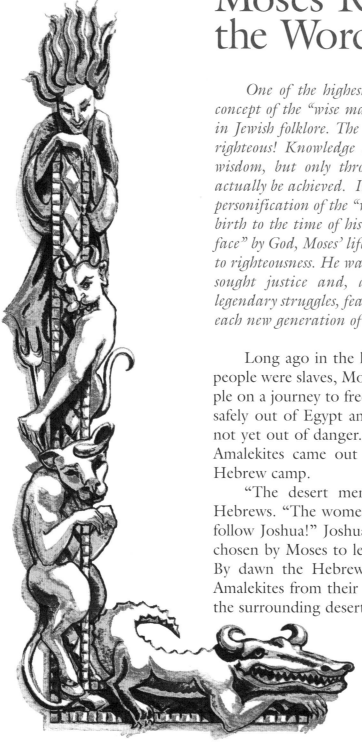

One of the highest ideals in Jewish tradition is the concept of the "wise man." It is found again and again in Jewish folklore. The "wise man" must be learned and righteous! Knowledge and reason can lead a person to wisdom, but only through great diligence can wisdom actually be achieved. In Jewish folk literature Moses is the personification of the "wise man." From the moment of his birth to the time of his death, when he was "kissed in the face" by God, Moses' life became a model for souls aspiring to righteousness. He was virtuous, had a passion for truth, sought justice and, above all, loved his people. His legendary struggles, feats, and victories continue to inspire each new generation of heroes.

Long ago in the land of Egypt, when the Hebrew people were slaves, Moses came forward to lead his people on a journey to freedom. Although he had led them safely out of Egypt and across the Red Sea, they were not yet out of danger. One night an army of nomadic Amalekites came out of the wilderness to attack the Hebrew camp.

"The desert men! The desert men!" cried the Hebrews. "The women and children to the hills! Men, follow Joshua!" Joshua was a young and fearless leader chosen by Moses to lead the Hebrew army into battle. By dawn the Hebrews had succeeded in driving the Amalekites from their camp, but the battle raged on in the surrounding desert.

Moses climbed to the top of a hill to observe the battle below and signal to his fighting men. When Moses held his arms high up in the air the Hebrews took control of the battle. When he lowered his arms to rest, however, the Amalekites took control again. Moses called to Arom and Hur to join him on the mountain. "We are losing!" he said. "Come, bring me a rock to sit on, and I would like each of you take one of my arms and hold it up in the air."

The sun beat down upon him, sweat rolled down his face, but Moses never moved. He sat perfectly still with his arms raised toward heaven. When the Hebrew soldiers looked up at the mountain and saw Moses, his beautiful white beard flowing in the wind, his arms raised toward heaven, they took courage and fought on.

All at once black clouds filled the sky, thunder roared, and rivers of rain began to fall, but Moses did not move. Just as he had withstood the scorching sun, he now braved the thunder and lightning and, with the help of Arom and Hur, kept his arms raised toward heaven.

"Courage, men!" cried Joshua. "One last charge and the desert men are no more. Onward! Onward!" By the time the rain stopped, and the sun sank below the hills, the Hebrews had conquered the Amalekites.

Moses' arms fell to his side, "My brothers, we shall be a great nation. We are no longer slaves. We are free! Let us build an altar to God."

Then Moses led his people through the wilderness. Each time the Hebrews met with danger a miracle occurred to save them. They never suffered from thirst or hunger. Moses told the people to gather bread each day. He taught them that on the sixth day they must gather enough bread for two days, so that they may spend the seventh day, the Sabbath, in prayer and worship of God.

Source ~ "Moses Receives the Word of God" is a legendary Biblical aggadah based on Exodus 19:3.

After a long journey through the desert, they came to a rich and fertile valley surrounded by tall, rugged mountains. At the foot of the most rugged mountain, Moses and the children of Israel set up their camp.

That night Moses called the leaders of the Hebrew tribes together and said, "The voice of God is calling me to the mountaintop to receive His Law. While I am gone I shall rely on you to care for my people."

Then Moses, with his staff in hand, left to climb the mountain by himself. The path was steep and sharp rocks cut Moses' feet. Overhead, the night sky turned black as great storm clouds gathered and a cold wind blew in from the north. Moses pulled his cloak closer around himself. When he reached the top of the mountain he was almost carried away by the brutal wind, but he felt God was near, and was not afraid.

With a flash of lightning brighter than daylight, the heavens opened and unleashed torrents of rain. Soaked and shivering with cold, Moses clung to a large over-hanging rock. A cloud that had been floating nearby abruptly stopped moving and parted to receive him. He stepped into it and rose up into the heavens.

The first being Moses met in heaven was the angel Kemuel, the leader of the Angels of Destruction. "What are you doing in these holy places?" demanded Kemuel, as he blocked Moses' path.

"I am the son of Amram," Moses replied, "I have come to receive the Torah for Israel." Kemuel laughed and refused to let him pass. Moses tried to push Kemuel out of the way, but Kemuel fought back. But Moses was stronger and destroyed Kemuel.

Moses continued on for sixty thousand leagues until he reached the post of the Angel Hadarniel. Whenever Hadarniel spoke, two lightning flashes accompanied each

word. Upon meeting Moses, his fiery voice bellowed out, "Who do you think you are that you dare come to this high holy realm?" Startled, and almost blinded by the accompanying lightning storm, Moses stumbled and almost fell from the cloud. Just then, the voice of the Holy and Blessed One was heard: "The angels do not want Me to give the Torah to Israel. They do not understand that if Israel does not receive the Torah there will never be a place on earth for Me."

This so shamed Hadarniel, that he asked God to allow him to serve as a guide for Moses. "I will go before him like a pupil goes before his master." And thus Hadarniel led Moses to the fires of Sandalphon. "I have authority to go only this far," said Hadarniel. "If I go farther the fire will consume me. Proceed on your own."

Frightened and alone, Moses saw no way to get through the fire. He cried out for help. The Holy and Blessed One answered, "Come, now you will see how dear Israel is to Me!" He then descended from the Throne of Glory and stood before the fires, shielding Moses until he had safely passed.

After he had cleared the fires of Sandalphon, Moses came to the River of Fire, whose boiling waters scorched angels and humans alike. But the Holy and Blessed One took hold of Moses and led him safely through the treacherous waters and into the chamber of the Throne of Glory.

There, seated around the Throne, were the great and mighty warrior angels. They wanted to burn Moses with their breath, but God spread his radiance on Moses. It protected him and enabled him to take his rightful place around the Throne. "Moses," said the Holy and Blessed One, "you have something to say to the angels — say it now."

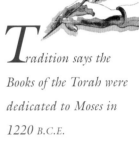

Tradition says the Books of the Torah were dedicated to Moses in 1220 B.C.E.

Tav **ת**, *the twenty-second and last letter of the alphabet, has a value of 400, and is the symbol of truth and perfection.*

The term Throne of Glory appears frequently in ancient Jewish literature in reference to God's throne.
— 2 CHRONICLES 18:18

187

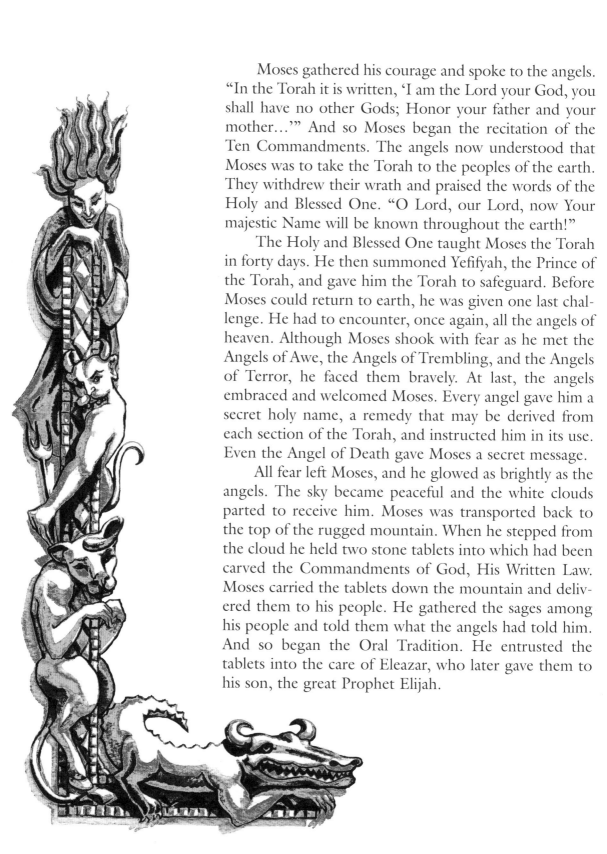

Moses gathered his courage and spoke to the angels. "In the Torah it is written, 'I am the Lord your God, you shall have no other Gods; Honor your father and your mother...'" And so Moses began the recitation of the Ten Commandments. The angels now understood that Moses was to take the Torah to the peoples of the earth. They withdrew their wrath and praised the words of the Holy and Blessed One. "O Lord, our Lord, now Your majestic Name will be known throughout the earth!"

The Holy and Blessed One taught Moses the Torah in forty days. He then summoned Yefifyah, the Prince of the Torah, and gave him the Torah to safeguard. Before Moses could return to earth, he was given one last challenge. He had to encounter, once again, all the angels of heaven. Although Moses shook with fear as he met the Angels of Awe, the Angels of Trembling, and the Angels of Terror, he faced them bravely. At last, the angels embraced and welcomed Moses. Every angel gave him a secret holy name, a remedy that may be derived from each section of the Torah, and instructed him in its use. Even the Angel of Death gave Moses a secret message.

All fear left Moses, and he glowed as brightly as the angels. The sky became peaceful and the white clouds parted to receive him. Moses was transported back to the top of the rugged mountain. When he stepped from the cloud he held two stone tablets into which had been carved the Commandments of God, His Written Law. Moses carried the tablets down the mountain and delivered them to his people. He gathered the sages among his people and told them what the angels had told him. And so began the Oral Tradition. He entrusted the tablets into the care of Eleazar, who later gave them to his son, the great Prophet Elijah.

Glossary

Aggadah   Literature of a legendary character in the Talmud and Midrash, including myths, legends, fables folktales, fairy tales, religious truths, and moral maxims. In a general sense, **aggadah** can refer to any legendary material found in Jewish literature.

gaon   A title of respect usually reserved for a scholarly genius.

Gemara   Rabbinical commentary, traditions, and discussions pertaining to the Mishnah in the Talmud. Gemara literally means "to study" in Aramaic.

Haggadah   A rabbinical text written two thousand years ago to commemorate the Jews' exodus to freedom. Additions to the text were made in the Middle Ages. The book is traditionally read at the Passover meal, the seder.

Halakha   Jewish law.

Hasidism   A mystical Jewish sect founded in Poland in the eighteenth century by Rabbi Israel ben Eliezer, the Baal Shem Tov. The members of the sect are **Hasidim**.

kabbalah   Mystical Jewish literature, or "secret doctrine." The central text of kabbalah is the Zohar, "Book of Splendor," attributed to the second-century Talmudic sage, Simeon bar Yohai, but revealed in the thirteenth century by Moshe de Leon.

kashrut   (adj. Kosher). The observance of Jewish dietary laws pertaining to permissible foods and food preparation.

Midrash   (1) A body of interpretive literature, devotional and ethical in character, that attempts to illuminate the inner meaning of the literal text of the Bible.
(2) A **midrash** (lower cased; pl. midrashim) is an individual midrashic legend.

Mishnah   The earliest doctrine of Jewish Oral Law.

mitzvah   (pl. mitzvot) Divine commandments that have come to mean "good deeds."

Sabbath   (**Shabbat** in Hebrew, **Shabbas** in Yiddish). Saturday, the sacred day.

Talmud   The Talmud is the most sacred Jewish text after the Bible. The Talmud's many volumes contain the Mishnah (Oral Law) and Gemara. The Palestinian, or Jerusalem, Talmud was completed in about 400 c.e., and the Babylonian Talmud was completed about a century later. Each has a different Gemara commenting on the same Mishnah.

Torah   The Five Books of Moses, the Bible (also, Pentateuch). It is referred to as the Old Testament, or the Written Law, and is the central document of Judaism.

tzaddik   (pl. tzaddikim). A title given to an unusually righteous man of God. Hasidim consider their religious leaders, called rebbes, to be tzaddikim.

Selected Bibliography

Ausubel, Nathan. *A Treasury of Jewish Folklore*. New York: Crown Publishers, 1974.

Ben Gorion, Micha Joseph. *Mimekor Yisrael Classical Jewish Folktales*. Bloomington and London: Indiana University Press, 1976.

Bettelheim, Bruno. *The Uses of Enchantment*. New York: Vintage Books, 1976.

Buber, Martin. *The Origin and Meaning of Hasidism*, trans. Maurice Friedman. New York: Horizon Press, 1960.

Carlgren, Frans. *Education Towards Freedom*. East Grinstead, England: Lanthorn Press, 1976.

Coles, Robert. *The Spiritual Life of Children*. Boston: Houghton Mifflin Company, 1990.

Cusick, Lois. *Waldorf Parenting Handbook*. Gainesville, Florida, 1979.

Encyclopaedia Judaica. Jerusalem, Israel: Keter Publishing House, Ltd., 1971.

Hadas, Moses. *Fox Fables of Berechiah ha-Nakdan*. New York: Columbia University Press, 1967.

Heuscher, Julius E. *A Psychiatric Study of Myths and Fairy Tales*. Springfield, Illinois: Charles C. Thomas, 1974.

Katz, Eli. *Book of Fables*. Detroit: Wayne University Press, 1994.

Kushner, Lawrence. *The Book of Letters, A Mystical Alef-bait*. Woodstock, Vermont: Jewish Lights, 1990.

Meter, Rudolf. *The Wisdom of Fairy Tales*. Great Britain: Floris Books, 1981.

Postman, Neil. *The Disappearance of Childhood*. New York: Delacourt Press, 1982.

Piaget, Jean. *Science of Education and the Psychology of the Child*. New York: Norton, 1970.

Rappoport, Angelo S. *Myth and Legend of Ancient Israel*. New York: KTAV Publishing House, 1966.

Rush, Barbara. *The Book of Jewish Women's Tales*. New Jersey: Jason Aronson, Inc. 1987.

Sader, Pinhas. *Jewish Folktales*. New York: Doubleday, 1989.

Schram, Peninnah. *Jewish Stories One Generation Tells Another*. New Jersey: Jason Aronson, Inc., 1987.

Schwartz, Howard. *Elijah's Violin and Other Jewish Fairy Tales*. New York: Harper and Row Publishers, 1983.

Steiner, Rudolf. *The Poetry and Meaning of Fairy Tales*. New York: Mercury Press, 1989.

Telushkin, Joseph. *Biblical Literacy*. New York: William Morrow and Co., Inc., 1997.

——. *Jewish Literacy*. New York: William Morrow and Co., Inc., 1991.

Tenenbaum, Samuel. *The Wise Men of Chelm*. New York: Thomas Goseloff, 1965.

Trachtenberg, Joshua. *Jewish Magic and Superstitions: A Study in Folk Religion*. New York: Beharman's Jewish Book House, 1939.

Vilnay, Zev. *Legends of Jerusalem*. Philadelphia: The Jewish Publication Society of America, 1973.

Von Franz, Marie Louise. *Interpretation of Fairytales*. Dallas: Spring Publications, 1970.

Weinreich, Beatrice & Wolf, Leonard. *Yiddish Folktales*. New York: Pantheon Books, 1988.

Index

PERMISSION ACKNOWLEDGMENTS

Chelsey Press gratefully acknowledges the following publishers for their permission to reprint:

Quote from *The Spiritual life of Children* by Robert Coles. Copyright © 1990, Houghton Mifflin Co.

Quote from *Jewish Stories One Generation Tells Another* by Peninnah Schram. Copyright © 1987, Jason Aronson, Inc., Northvale, NJ.

Derivations of "Lion, Mouse, Snare," "Dog, Cheese, Water," from *Fables of a Jewish Aesop, Translated from the Fox Fables of Berechiah ha-Nakdan,* by Moses Hadas. Copyright © 1967, Columbia University Press.

Derivations of "Stones and Bones Rattle in My Belly," "The Naughty Little Girl," "The Golem of Vilna," "The Orphan Boy Who Won the Bride," from *Yiddish Folktales* by Beatrice Weinreich-Silverman, translated by Leonard Wolf. Copyright © 1988, YIVO Institute for Jewish Research. Pantheon Books, a division of Random House, Inc.

Derivation of "Who Cured the Princess?" from *Folktales of Israel* edited by Dov Noy. Copyright © 1963, University of Chicago Press.

Derivation of "The Birds Which Turned to Stone" from *Legends of Jerusalem* by Zev Vilnay. Copyright © 1973, The Jewish Publication Society of America.

Derivation of "The Angel's Wings" *from The Diamond Tree: Jewish Tales from Around the World* by Howard Schwartz and Barbara Rush. Copyright © 1991, Harper Collins Publishers.

Derivations from *A Child's History of the Hebrew People* by Dorothy F. Zeligs. Copyright © 1940. Permission granted by Charles Bloch, Bloch Publishing Co., New York.

SPECIAL ACKNOWLEDGMENT

"The Story of Ruth" and "The Two Brothers" have been adapted from stories in *Haderech*, a magazine edited by S. B. Unsdorfer, and are included in this collection in honor of his memory and as a tribute to his contribution of fine literature for children. Unsdorfer's books include *Stories of Simcha* and *The Yellow Star*.